THIS MIND IS RESTLESS FOR NIGERIA

(a dispatch and collection about Nigeria in the eyes of the author)

Chukwuemeka D. Azubuike

Dedication

I am dedicating this book to my family; my wife (Ego Oyibo) Amaka; for your patience, understanding and equally making the home more conducive for my various postulations about Nigeria. To my parents Chief & Lolo Nicholas Osuagwu who laid the foundation of a good education that equipped my mind to undertake this onerous task of writing and to my sisters (Nne, Ify and Amy) who truly have become the strength and inspiration to keep walking and working on my strong convictions about life and Nigeria.

To the Nigerian youth who keeps grinding, working and hustling to create the future we have long desired. We shall all thrive together as countrymen and women.

Acknowledgment

This is to appreciate everyone who has in one way contributed to my growth and development; who truly believed in my purpose for living. I equally want to appreciate my friend and the editor Cincin Akanya who has spent personal finances, time, effort and resources editing my writing and endlessly ideas about Nigeria. She truly saw something that I myself have not seen.

1. A NATION OF SABOTEURS

The story of Nigeria and saboteurs reminds me of the story of Achan in the biblical account of the Israelites attacking the city of Jericho and Ai but was defeated by the latter due to the action of one man in the former. In brief, Achan decided to disobey an instruction not to take anything belonging to the city they attacked and that caused them to be defeated by the next city they attacked. The sin of one man affected a whole nation.

The peculiarity of ours is that we have many people acting as one (saboteur) in one area, sector, industry, ministry, department, and agency. It really causes heartache knowing that while some people desire a better nation, some others are working against it. The news headlines are not helpful in making one be hopeful for the future and where we are going. We have been on potential stage for over 50 years. Isn't it bad enough that we still produce just about 1600 MW of electricity for well over 170 million people? South Africa produces about 40,000 MW for about 50 million people.

What can we possibly achieve with such distribution level of electricity, what kind of industry can we actually build with that?

The reason for such level of power distribution by the Nigerian Electricity Regulatory Commission is the vandalism of power facilities and this affects the gas level needed to provide power and this yet is sabotage by people who don't know this affects every one of us. This same trend is seen highly in the public sector, the private sector, on the streets, car parks, churches, mosques, etc. We can have people employed to clean the streets and get paid yet you will find people who still take pleasure in littering the same streets as they are being cleaned. We also have people who see destroying facilities like the streets lights or light poles as a worthy way to get back to the government or whoever they think is the cause of their woes and challenges.

It seems like we are all running the wrong direction, everyone with a sole vision or goal of amassing wealth for themselves, family no matter how it is done; even if it impoverishes the next person. In the midst of anything genuine, there is fake in this country. Drugs are being counterfeited, water, clothes, software, computer applications, watches, electronics, books; even systems are being corrupted and replaced by something dubious and of low standards. The roads awarded to contractors or buildings are constructed badly for the sake of making profits not caring about the big picture of building something that can outlive generations.

This same attitude is also seen in government where people work against the goodwill and policies of either the president or governors irrespective of party affiliations. People now think that their individual or group interests supersede those of every Nigerian and Nigeria. They lay claim to the Commonwealth of the nation and are willing to do anything to keep having access to it no matter who is dying or suffering from such irresponsible and irresponsive actions.

Talking about actions, we also have the challenge of inaction where people decide to do nothing when they have the power to actually do something. Every state government should know that running a government based on revenue generated from tax alone is not sustainable yet they maintain the status quo. This is also is sabotage of not only the people who elected you but of your own conscience because at the end the excuse we get is in the payment of salaries due to limited revenues which you had the ability to actually do something about.

There are many areas of sabotage in the project called Nigeria. We are not yet working as one and unfortunately, this has prolonged because the many arrays of leaders and government have refused to carry everyone along and develop a comprehensive plan that will focus everyone on a goal we can actually call a Nigerian Dream. We sure need a Nigerian Dream, a vision, direction, a common goal that will define the action and inaction of everyone.

The best way to address sabotage is to bring everyone to the table and find the elements of grievance and see if we can to an extent assuage everyone's fear of discrimination, prejudice, hate and most importantly create a sense of belonging for every Nigerian. This is a core duty of the government and leadership at all levels.

2. A TALE OF THE MMM SCHEME AND MORE

I was caught up between making this piece one of sarcasm, truth or anger but for the sake of reason, respect, and mutual love for our country I intend to make everyone share in the blame for it. It is a well-known fact by now that the many schemes that are springing up every week are all Ponzi schemes. Personally, I was ignorant about them up until 2015 when I came back from a work that took me far north when I was invited for 5 of such schemes in less than 4 months. I must confess it was scary and tricky because I almost started thinking maybe that's where my opportunity lies for a breakthrough.

I won't try to justify myself or exonerate myself from it or pretend as if I was not tempted to join, I was but eventually participated in one, cashed out my profits without further reinvesting in it. With my little experience in website design, I was too sure that those websites especially MMM was shaky, unstable and would one day result in bad stories (at least not yet fully told).

Do you know that there were people who put 2 million naira in the MMM scheme and some did it twice and more and little wonders why such an amount cannot be invested in a business, run, grow it and build something that can create jobs, add value and also increase our GDP, taxes and many other benefits. Of course, that has not been the case especially since the nation slid into a recession that seems to be crippling everything and uncertainties are high. So you can really blame someone that puts his money where within 2 weeks he can get some interest in it.

Nigeria as a nation that should be creating opportunities for people to dream and live their dream has only offered hopelessness and despair. The leadership is self-centred, greedy, corrupt, and all these, in turn, tell on their abilities to think creatively about how to meet our many challenges. Our leaders are from what Napoleon Bonaparte said about leaders who should be 'dealers in hope' rather they are dashing hopes every day.

What this has created is a lack of trust in the system; socio-economic and political environment. The rule of hard work and reaping rewards no longer apply here, natural laws of success are simply myths because the configuration called Nigeria does not support it.

So I guess, the government of many years should be blamed for all that but does that justify the actions of the citizenry?

I don't think so! Values are not meant to be practised when everything is working out but the strength of one's values is determined in hard times. This, of course, varies with people and everyone knows his or her own level of accountability especially to themselves. This decadence in our value system can be blamed on a number of reasons and leadership failure will be at the top of it.

The suffering in the land is much, inflation is high, the system works against businesses, whatever challenges we have in this country I can say are all man-made and that is most unfortunate indeed. Nations with natural disasters are doing well in managing the external factors while still being in full control of what they can influence; unfortunately, it is not so in this part of the world.

If Nigeria and those who it is their responsibility to create a system that works for everyone (irrespective of any social stratification), then people will continue getting involved in schemes they feel will serve their economic interests even when they look fraudulent. If someone knows that starting a business can work for him in 3 to 6 months then there won't be a need to enter schemes like MMM after all, Nigerians are not close to being lazy at work but if it is otherwise then such schemes will keep getting lots of patronage from Nigerians.

We are either offering hope or dashing hopes which will keep creating more desperation in our citizens.

3. THOUGHTS ON NCC SIM REGISTRATION DIRECTIVE

For some time now I have been thinking about the efficiency of the compulsory registration of mobile line number for our phones. It all started as a directive by the NCC to all service providers to register their customers and that involved one giving out some details about themselves. It sounded more like another clamour to get the National Identity Cards or more recently the Permanent Voters' Card. In any case, all I can say is that the exercise is a failure considering the fact that we have been told to go back a second time yet no improvement was made to the previous process.

A few weeks back I came back to the shocking news that one of my neighbours has been waylaid of a whooping sum of 1.2 million naira by a taxi driver she exchanged numbers with. Driving my point without much ado, she tried tracking the number and a foreign name appeared as the name used to register the SIM card. Also, the mobile operators for the SIM card couldn't track the identity or location of the person involved. What then is the purpose of the SIM registration; is it just for having the statistics of mobile phones users or there is more the citizens don't know of?

The process of registration is not new to any mobile phone users or even an adolescent, so I will go over it briefly. You get to the independent officers doing the registration and the ask you some basic questions; names, mother's maiden name, address, phone number, date of birth, state and local governments of origin, picture portrait of the user and so on. The unfortunate thing is that there is no basis for verifying the information entered by anyone; no ID, no database, or whatsoever. In fact, the fingerprints collected are not used for anything in particular. Why do I say that?

People who do fraud with their SIM cards do so easily because one person can buy as many SIM cards anywhere (which is wrong), register as many as possible with different names and start using it to do all kinds of atrocities. If the fingerprint database was useful or properly implemented, it will be easy to backtrace such a person based on a particular location, state, age or any similar information. So if a person comes and says he is from a particular state and local government, rather scan the database of over 50 million people, you can easily narrow down your search to the information he/she provides.

I remember a blogger suggesting that an easy way to tackle the insurgents in the North-East is by ensuring everyone has a National ID card so we all can verify our citizenship as Nigerians. These processes have gone on forever yet no substantial deployment of these technologies has been achieved. Identity cards can be used to check crime, corruption, financial indiscipline and what have you, yet we keep on bringing up processes that will torment the ordinary Nigerian and more cash released to be sabotaged by a few people.

We really need to get certain things right before some others can work correctly or better still achieve their purposes. The good book says if the foundation is destroyed what can the righteous do? I am aware that a new technology thrives on previous ones so rather than waste resources on a good idea that has no foundation to take off, let us try and get it first before proceeding to the next one. The news is everywhere on how the National Communication Commission has fined a mobile operator for this same processes that have not been used to even curb crime in our society. Isn't the hypocrisy too much for one nation to bear?

If our institutions cannot work to design a workable system that can make the society safer and also work optimally what then can they really do? Every one of our institutions is being privatized; are those who will be working in the private institutions better in thinking than those who used to work there? These are pertinent questions that require satisfactory and truthful answers for those who make policies for us and at the same time subject Nigerians to the rigours of long queues in the same process over and over again.

If this registration process was good enough that my neighbour would have easily located the person who hypnotized and took away her millions but because the thief has been able to register a SIM with another name that is not even Nigerian, he got away with it. I wonder the nature of crimes being committed by this flaw in our system.

God help us all!

4. THE NEXT GENERATION OPPORTUNIST

No matter the decadence and the altitude of the altars of corruption in the African continent, I am too sure and highly optimistic that the future holds something better and sustainable for our Nations. Evil can only prevail for a while and the events of today is a fight between light and darkness and the obvious will always happen. Africa as a continent is passing through tough times today, we are the ones that all the aids come to, and we are the victims of ethnic wars and violence but all these are happening so that as a continent we would have a story to tell. ***A story*** *of independence, of hope, one that led us through trial times, in disagreement with one another until we get to one of prosperity for posterity.* It will be on record that we survived the toughest and fiercest level of violence. It will also prove that we have been able to develop political structures and systems that can't be found anywhere in the world. For instance, Nigeria will be proud to say they developed and built a democracy that now accommodates over 400 ethnic groups equally, with a collective goal and vision.

Yes, the opposition seems to be strong and all-powerful but I see an army of reformers and Nation builders rising. An army of disciplined men and women of character and skill. They might be small in number but it only reminds me of George Washington's quote that, "Discipline is the soul of an army, it makes small numbers formidable and procures esteem to all". *Good men of like minds are always committed to a cause and work together but evil men will always disagree when overtaken by their own greed and avarice to overtake one another.*

There is a willing and able generation rising to restore our dignity as a continent but oppositions will abound also. People also would work against the reforms. These people are those who feel they can continue to perpetuate the deeds of the past generation. Men and women who would operate with a mindset that if our fathers did it, why can't we do same. Those are the next generation opportunists who will take corruption to a whole new level that is not even present now. It is said that evil prevails when good men do nothing. So as they improve their dubious means, it is up to the good ones to raise a standard to fight and combat them at any level.

We can't afford to repeat the mistakes of history or tread the path of turning a blind eye while evil thrives. It will be a head-on collision of good and evil and darkness will always give way to light. Keeping quiet and playing safe in our comfort zone will do no good but hunt us even in that comfort zone. Rather than being cowards in our closets, is better to act in courage, pay the price and take the enemy in a battle that our Nations might live.

In only a matter of decades, our children will begin to weigh and judge us and criticize us on social media (futuristic ones) as men who sat on the fence, shied away from taking action, abated evil men or men who stood for the truth and made tangible and lasting contributions for posterity to be sure.

Africa must rise!!!

5. AS RED MEDIA AFRICA CHAMPIONS THE CHANGE MANTRA

It looks as if there is a sweeping change mantra across the world as ruling parties are losing elections to the opposition parties and no continent is left behind as the great nation of America experienced same recently. Nigeria took the lead in voting out a party that swore to be in power for 60 years but only was voted out after a bad outing of 16 years. For Nigeria, you can say that what used to be the rejected stone became the face of change because the people spoke alongside many other factors involved.

It was a hard-fought campaign that didn't focus on the real issues with a large media publicity that has never been experienced before. Social media played a critical role and many other modern-day trends were brought to bear; especially on the Public Relations aspect of it.

Behind the scenes of the All Progressives Congress campaign of President Buhari was a media organization that now prides itself as the voice of the millennial generation and more recently for taking back power to the people. Red Media Africa; the owners of YNaija, The Future Awards Africa, Rubbing Minds of ChannelsTV and other media outfits have proved their worth when it comes to the contemporary media business. I will also like to say that I admire the brand and in fact when I was planning to start my magazine, YNaija was the first magazine I got long before I knew about the configuration of the brand.

The co-founder of the company Red Media Africa, Debola Williams is at the forefront of talking about the brand. This was in the event of the defeat of the ruling party in Ghana, where he posted on his Instagram page about the role they played in that election while adding the need to return power to the people. The first question I would ask is, Has Red Media become partisan in being part of the campaign party or are they simply fulfilling business needs and expectations? Interestingly there were reactions to

@DebolaLagos post on Instagram especially on the part they played in bringing the now unpopular government of President Buhari to power.

Going further, the Nigerian government has become somewhat unpopular because of their economic policies that seem to be causing more sufferings for the people. Red Media Africa, on the other hand, seems to be making President Buhari "the man of the hour" when things are actually hard to the people.

With that said, can they (Red Media Africa) after championing the change of returning power back to the people still come out and condemning seemingly wrong moves, actions, inactions, and policies of these governments they helped put in power. Yes! they are a media company and should be less partisan but can their interest in running a campaign and endorsements that are dropped sometimes really mean business alone? Being actively involved in sacking a particular party in power, does it make them business-minded alone or also partisan seeing that they actually pitched a tent with one party?

A new government has been elected in Ghana and Red Media was part of the campaign; if by tomorrow or let's say the next 18 months that the government becomes unpopular due to unfulfilled promises to the people of Ghana, will Red Media still claim they gave back power to the people?

These are rhetorics that definitely won't need a direct answer but we have to tell ourselves the truth and also say such truth to a government that seems to be losing focus on the mark of their leadership. Winning parties can one day become losers in governance and we owe it to the people we serve (as the media) to tell the truth no matter what business relationships that might have been built in the past.

What will it be, Business or Truth?

6. FEDERALISM IS SPIRITUAL

It is the system of governance that makes use of regionalism, federating units, states and a neutral centre to administer the work of government. The essence as always has been to create a form of autonomy for different regions and states.

It creates a competitive and balanced government that benefits both the regional and the central government. Federalism decentralizes power and shares it with smaller units of governance.

Based on the good book, Deut. 1:10-17 is a picture of what administering effective leadership by maximizing shared responsibilities should be. Moses recognized the increase in number and population of the Israelites i.e. complexity of behaviours among the people he is leading. Responsibilities will be more and it will be cumbersome for one person or a central government to administer alone.

Verse 13, you can see Moses telling the people to take wise men and understanding among their tribes to rule over them and they welcomed it (v.14). He made them heads and captains of thousands, hundreds, the fifties and tens. They were now to hear causes among them and judge righteously. At the end, he told them to bring the difficult cases to him.

This to me describes delegation and federalism. This time more leaders are chosen and a group of people given to them to rule. It removes the tension and strife that might occur at the central government. In it, more progress is made and each leader tends to achieve more. They are able to administer and manage resources judiciously and efficiently.

Finally, in federalism, if the regional government can't handle some issues, programs and projects, the central government would intervene in such cases. Moses also charged his new leaders with this admonition. In it, we achieve more with little success.

7. BILL GATES: MYTHS ABOUT DROPPING OUT OF UNIVERSITY

He is one man who has risen to become a household name in the world both as computer entrepreneur to a philanthropist who is investing his wealth in making the world a better place. Has been ranked severally as the world richest man and so many things have been said about his story of success.

One of such stories is that he dropped out Harvard University after his sophomore year to start his own software company. Now when people make reference to this, they make it seem that people can actually make a jest of education, drop out and go on to start a business or do what they actually love. While it is seen that Bill Gates dropped of college, we must also not forget that he didn't stop learning or educating himself. Leaving a school system doesn't mean one has stopped learning or being educated.

Way back before entering Harvard or even thinking of dropping out, as an eighth grader in 1968, Bill Gates taught himself how to program and according to him, he spent so many hours on the computer with his friends. They ran about 1575 hours on the computer which equals about 8 hours a day, 7 days a week. He said it was like an obsession, they skipped athletics and spent time learning to programme, even late into the night. (Malcolm Gladwell, The Outliers)

His mother recounting said, they wondered why he found it difficult to wake up in the morning. He was burning his midnight candles doing what he loved and wanted to explore and venture into. By the time he dropped out of Harvard to start his company he had programmed for 7 years. So he has schooled and educated himself; building the needed capacity to launch out as a computer entrepreneur.

In school, we are given lectures, deadlines are set for assignments and must be met if you are ever going to pass or graduate. There is a demand on you to deliver and for Bill, he already consciously gave himself that task of losing sleep to learn something new. At that point, you could say he has gone past the mastery level with over 10,000 hours invested in those seven years.

Now that is the story of Bill Gates long before the decision to drop out Harvard University.

Asides him there are many other people who when their stories are told, we are quick to make reference to the fact that they dropped out of school; people like Thomas Edison, Richard Branson and the rest. We need to stop passing the wrong message to younger generations by telling the real success story; the story of hard work, the time, the efforts, the sleepless nights, the rejections, the failures; that these people had to go through before a break could be achieved.

It won't be fair to sell a hatred for education because we feel the school system is poorly structured. That people like Gates didn't fancy the school system doesn't mean he also abhors learning and getting educated or building capacity needed to run his business.

8. BUDGET SIGNING CONTROVERSY AND OUR NATIONAL CONSCIENCE

After a long-drawn controversy that characterized the 2016 Appropriation Bill (Budget 2016), the National Assembly finally passed the document into law. The drama was in the form of budget padding and inclusion of more details different from what President Buhari presented late last year.

As is the nature of any democracy, the President is expected to assent to the budget so it can take effect for 2016 fiscal year. In his wisdom and good judgment, the President gave a condition to see the budget details before his assent. This also created a further media debate and hype with most citizens giving the President a pass mark on that while some are howling at him for delaying further.

The House Committee Chairman on Appropriation, Abdulmumin Jibrin had this to say, "In order for the nation to move forward and avoid stagnation of administrative processes, the tradition is that the bill is passed and forwarded to the presidency for assent, while the lawmakers continue to work on the details. There is nothing abnormal about this practice and yet nothing abnormal about a president accenting a budget before or after seeing the details. In any case, the budget details are usually sent within a week or two after passing the budget."

If you are this post or have access to a smartphone or ever filled a form online you will be familiar with Terms of Agreement. This common and popular document is always waived off by almost everyone that comes across it. We all are guilty of agreeing or signing terms we have not even read through.

One would have thought that kind of attitude should be left online and for internet agreements and contracts, but unfortunately, we have displayed this in dealing with a vital document as the National Budget. For legislators to be making assertions that the President signing the budget before or after seeing the details is irrelevant is highly shameful for our national conscience.

Do you go into a partnership business without reading the deeds of partnership? Yet a lawmaker or lawmakers think it right to sign the budget without perusing the details. We have also seen situations where people sign their tenancy agreements without reading through and when a dispute comes up you find out they don't have an idea of what they signed.

In these modern times, your signature is like an oath. Covenant or access; that is the only thing that guarantees your ability to have access to your money lodged in a bank. So it carries a lot of weight and here we are expecting our Commander-in-Chief to sign a document like the budget without looking at the details.

If tomorrow there are discrepancies in it he will still share in the blame, in fact, most of it. We need some purging of our national conscience if we want to build a strong and viable Nigeria. People forget the budget documents are legal documents and legal issues demand compliance with the law. Some laws don't need to be stated before you know it is the right thing to do and this scenario is one of such.

With a pure conscience, the easiest of common senses and hard conviction, President Muhammadu Buhari has the presidential rights to demand the details of that budget before accents. In fact, he has gone further to give the Office of the President a moral and facelift by not doing just anything.

9. THE OBJECTIVITY & SUBJECTIVITY OF THE WORD IN LEADERSHIP

Leadership all through the ages and of human civilization has proved to be the bedrock of change, influence, social and economic development. It is what determines the outcome of families, groups, organizations and Nations. Whenever something is not working optimally, the first point of reference is the leadership; what have they done, in what direction and what can they do to be better.

It is commonly described as influencing a group of people, families, organizations and Nations in achieving a worthwhile goal. In essence, it involves an influencer or leader and the followers or a team. The greatest leader that lived and passed through this world, our Lord Jesus

Christ portrayed rare leadership virtues. His style of leadership was comprehensive and dynamic. Jesus was a servant leader (washing the feet of the disciples), at some point, he had to be authoritative/ autocratic (in flogging the people from the temple), at some point bureaucratic (give to Caesar what belongs to Caesar); in fact. He was a true reflection of dynamism in leadership. The ultimate goal or essence of His leadership was that after His sojourn of about 3 years in ministry, men and people were transformed i.e. His dynamism in other leadership styles resulted in transformational leadership or outcome.

The Word of God, the Bible is a book of truths, mysteries, ideas, power and in fact, a wise man said it is the oldest book with the latest news. It is in the application in all areas of life, through all ages, under any circumstances, no verse in this Book has a private interpretation (2Pet. 1:20-21). It is, therefore, a dynamic book that can address any need of mankind. This talks therefore about the objectivity and subjectivity of the Word. I will be focusing on drawing light from the Word on leadership today. This old rugged book can and still addresses issues of leadership in this 21st century.

One of the greatest concepts of leadership I have been privileged to be taught about is in Jud. 9:8-15.This talks about the trees who wanted to anoint a king (leader) and the olive tree were appointed to lead and it said, "Should I leave my fatness, wherewith by me they honour God and man and go to be promoted over trees? They went ahead to the fig tree asking it reign over them and the fig tree said; "Should I forsake my sweetness and my good fruit, and go to be promoted over the trees? The vine was also given this opportunity to lead and it said; "Should I leave my vine, which cheers God and go to be promoted over the trees?

Then they approached the bramble, Come thou and reign over us. The bramble said to the trees if in truth ye anoint me king over you then come and put your trust in my shadow, and if not, let fire come out of the bramble, devour the cedars of Lebanon. A great story isn't it?

The first three trees (olive, fig and vine) were concerned more about adding value than occupying a leadership position. They were happy to be making lives better with what they have and also content and satisfied with it. From the trees, we understand you don't need a position to influence people but a heart for people, one that longs to see people become better than they were. You can still be in the remotest place or village and impact the lives of people. The good book says when there is no vision (leadership) my people perish (Pro.29:18). Leadership is less of the leader but more of the people. The people are the essence and subject of leadership and should be a major beneficiary.

Still, on the trees, they proceeded to the bramble, come reign over us. This small tree said that the other big trees should come and put their trust in it and its shadows and if not let fire from it consume the cedars of Lebanon. Bad and irresponsible leadership comes because men and women who don't value themselves are entrusted with a huge task to care for others. The bramble, in essence, wanted other trees reduced to its level, he wanted to be their lord, and he wanted only to be the best among them while they are reduced to nothing.

Let's get more subjective and objective here.

The above illustration about the trees can be likened to the politics of present-day Nigeria and Africa. One where the leaders want everyone to be under them by incessant abuse of power and authority. Leaders who ask us to go to hospitals, schools and places they won't go ask their children to. These people are focused on what they will get; their prestige and well-being against adding value, uplifting lives when it is obvious that Africa is in the vestibule of change and in dire need of it also.

What Africa needs at this point in her history are people that can be likened to the fig tree, vine and olive trees, who are concerned more with adding value, who lead change without occupying any position, men and women of like minds that will act based on their convictions with the truth not just public opinion.

King David, who today is still celebrated in Israel, was indeed a man after God's own heart. He longed to please God every day, yes, even though he fell to temptation sometimes, he had the good conscience to come back and ask for mercy. A repentant heart and a man of skill and integrity. The man David as described in Ps. 78:72 led God's people first by the integrity of his heart; he had a clear conscience, one that puts God first in all circumstances and by the skillfulness of his hand. He was a shepherd boy, a songwriter and skilful player of the harp.

He had track records of results or antecedents of successes before confronting Goliath as a shepherd boy.

A man should not be given the opportunity to lead until he has proved himself worthy of little things, someone who has been able to achieve success, not from governmental booties, corruption and fraud. Politics today is like a business especially in Africa but the life of David tells us of a man who was diligent in keeping the sheep with all seriousness, zeal, valour and wholeheartedly. David on his deathbed confessed by the move of the Spirit that leading men must be in the fear of God, talking about justice and integrity. Leadership and integrity go hand in hand and its importance cannot be overemphasized. Pro. 11:3, talks about how a man's integrity will guide him i.e. his actions are controlled by it, it protects him from evil because his enemies will love him. 2Sam. 23:13-17, narrates of how David yearned to have a drink and when he cried out, his men rushed to the camp of the Philistines (three of them), i.e. they risked their lives that a good leader can live. A good man will always have people speak out for him, defend him in his absence and also willing to die for him.

I wonder if such a thing can happen in Nigeria and Africa today amongst our politicians. Imagine them walking on a street filled with disgruntled citizens, guess the answer to that question is obviously obvious.

Nehemiah, a cupbearer and exile in a strange land was committed to the work of restoring glory in his homeland rather than feed on the pays, food and entitlements of the governor. He also made sure that his subordinates (ministers and governors) did same. Their entitlements were given back to the people. He never robbed them once. (Neh. 5:14-18)

Daniel was relevant in a strange land for 60 years. Every government needed him to solve problems for them. He was a man of knowledge, who understood by books, a spiritual man who cares more about God's opinion against the opinions of the kings of Babylon. In Africa, is it possible to see men/ women stand up against a president/governor when he is getting it wrong; who will tell the truth that is most evident, not hypocrites and men with an evil conscience? Despite all, I know there are such men, good men/ women who love this continent, but they need to start speaking against evil. It shouldn't be allowed to thrive when the good still lives.

The Word of God is the best book I have come across; rich in the truth i.e. everything therein is relevant and will continue to be till Jesus comes. Facts can become obsolete but the truth shall be forever. It is applicable to life situations and leadership is one of such area.

Leadership is key to any meaningful transformation; once the head is corrupt the whole body would be too. Africa needs such leaders right now; not a crowd just a man in some cases who will groom others and make them be like he is. In leadership, I believe a tree can actually make a forest; just a man on fire for God can confront and bring down every networks and altar of corruption.

10.   POLITICAL LEADERS' INFLUENCE AND FOLLOWERS' REACTIONS

Leadership, as it has been practised, is such that a leader will no longer be one if he actually has no one following or someone he is influencing. A wise man once said that if you are leading and no one is following, then you are only taking a stroll. Likewise, the world will be even more chaotic if people who will lead are lacking i.e. everyone is doing what he/she feels is right in their eyes.

The idea is that a leader needs someone to influence and the follower needs some direction, inspiration, motivation and someone to rally them around towards a common objective. Influence I will say works both ways; a leader thinks he is influencing someone and the follower also thinking that he is doing what the leader will advise.

What of a situation where there is a misinterpretation of the thoughts of both the leader and follower? I will shed more light on that.

In Nigeria for instance, after the 2011 general elections where Muhammadu Buhari of the defunct Congress for Progressive Change lost to the Peoples Democratic Party candidate, Goodluck Jonathan. The outcome of that election resulted in violence that was caused either by the supporters of both candidates who perhaps thought they were doing the bidding of their candidates. These candidates will still come out, address their supporters and urge them not to react or panic but rather ensure social order even though they go on to do otherwise. Now at this point, you will agree that that influence of a leader over the follower is obviously missing.

That is simply just one ideal scenario where we have followers acting in a manner that the leader will speak against. This is a big challenge though especially in political leadership unlike a one-one mentoring that a leader will give to his protégé. This same development was seen in the just concluded American election where people took to the streets to protest the outcome of the election that made Donald Trump a President-Elect and the would-be 45th President of the United States. Those people most likely would be the supporters of Hillary Clinton who feel they were acting in the interest of the American people and the former secretary of state.

And if a Hillary Clinton is interviewed on that action, she will most likely speak against creating social unrest and probably tell them to accept the outcome and let the nation move forward.

Leadership is such an onerous task especially when you are in the driver's seat and the buck stops with you. As much as being answerable to your followers is part of being a leader, sometimes you have to take responsibility for their actions including their misdeeds. After all, you are the inspiration they see and they try to pattern their lives as they see you live. There might not be a direct solution to this disparity of opinion and action between leaders and followers because some followers will boast in the name of their leader and even go to the extent of committing crimes because they feel they can get away with it.

How then do you fix this?

This can be difficult like I said but for the leader not to get into trouble by what his followers do in his acceptance, he needs to do the following;

- He must learn to communicate and speak to the public and address those who hold him in high esteem.
- The leader should learn to address misconceptions, opinions, assumptions and ideas by coming out to clear the air and making his personal and leadership stand known.
- Of importance also, is for the leader to be consistent in his philosophies, ideologies and whatever he stands for. It will be unfortunate and

embarrassing for a leader to be changing position on issues when called upon.

- He also should be prompt to condemn wrong especially if is perpetuated by those who claim to be admiring him/her.

As a leader you must realize that people will second guess you and in fact assume the actions they think you will take; it will be good for you to be known for something. Let your thoughts be well known and if possible documented so that no questions will be asked later.

11.   HOW THE KNOWLEDGE ECONOMY IS COSTING US AN INDUSTRIAL AGE

How excited I was when I heard my entrepreneurship professor mention that man has gradually moved away from heavy equipment, manufacturing and activities that require the use of physical strength, to what is now known as a knowledge economy. He started out his lecture by saying "Idea is business." My excitement came from the fact that I was making strides in my new found love of writing and creating blog posts that have never been read by anyone.

It is always a good feeling to know people are reading your intellectual creation and also giving positive feedback.

The time before this century was regarded as the industrial age where heavy equipment and manufacturing was the mainstay of many economies. The nations were tapping into the inventions of scientists and inventors to build roads, bridges, and many infrastructures we see today. Their works involved knowledge application but less emphasis was laid on data, storage and processing them but today we have data storage and analysis, sharing, applications, and over time they can be updated to meet up with present-day challenges.

The knowledge economy is light in nature because data and knowledge can today be stored in small storage devices in their thousands and conveniently carried about. Meanwhile, the industrial age was raw m heavy and complicated. It will be worthy to note that these two eras are related and this will form the basis for my argument and assertion.

What are the elements or features of a knowledge economy?

The elements of a knowledge economy are created from the research works that were discovered and implemented industries and these can include;

- Personal Computers
- Laptops
- Projectors
- Pens
- Pencils
- Smartphones
- Tablets
- Modems
- USB cables
- Computer hardware equipment
- Printers
- Photocopiers
- Technical drawing equipment

Others which require technical know-how to operate especially in the field can include;

- Bulldozers

- Caterpillars
- Mixers
- Generators
- Inverters, etc.

The elements that drive the knowledge economy of today are enormous and can be found in many African economies like Nigeria, not developed by us but mostly imported from developed countries. You can see this in the fashion industry where we now design and make our own clothing; thanks to African designers, but the bad news is that the sewing machines, printers and all others are not produced in our economies.

Nigeria and other African nations skipped the opportunity to develop our homemade industries rather we focused more on exported raw materials and natural resources without making efforts to explore them. Some say we experience a brain drain while the colonialists were around, what happened after they left? Didn't we have some of our people going abroad to study, sponsored by the government or their kinsmen? Why didn't we learn the skills and know-how of production and industrialization, rather all we did was to learn the bureaucracies of politics and how to use it for personal gains and thievery.

These have gone on for far too long and in recent times it has been proved that those who explore raw materials for end-products sake are the winners. They are there to service those who can't produce and make them feel that they are now in a knowledge economy where things are done differently. Oil is crashing and Nigeria is wailing but if we were involved in petrochemicals and other end products of oil, we won't have a need to complain because we would have products that will continue to sell.

The situation is quite unfortunate because no one and I mean no one will be concerned about investing in research work to produce the elements that now drive these knowledge economies. We have iron ore, columbite, tin and a lot more but we prefer to keep importing what others have done and made easy for us. The wealthy or those that have oil blocks to their names rather continue importation than sponsoring a research to explore the Nigerian crude and what it can offer in its most finished state.

In every ecosystem there are producers and consumers, givers and takers, lenders and borrowers; in all these one is master over the other. The economic system of the world has been structured in such a way that some are producing what they need and also feeding it other nations who can't (that is justifiable) or won't produce despite an abundance of resources.

As much as we admire this knowledge economy, it is better we drive it by ourselves, with our products because we have the potential to and the capacity can be built if we are ready. That might be the only way for our currency to survive in a highly competitive market.

12.　　ROCHAS: IN SURPASSING THE WORKS OF DEE SAM

In his first inaugural speech as governor of Imo State Owelle Rochas Okorocha boldly proclaimed to Imolites that he would break the records of Sam Mbakwe, who was the first executive governor of Imo State. Most of the infrastructures that are now dilapidated in the state were done in his time as governor and he is one man history will continue to remember, not only in Imo but Nigeria as a whole.

Owelle Rochas was well embraced by Imo people when in 2011 he defeated an incumbent to emerge as governor. No doubt his humanitarian efforts created a good image for him in the hearts of many but one thing I have learnt is in political leadership you require more than just your goodwill to run and manage a people with diverse needs and challenges. Imolites reposed a lot of confidence in him like never before. When he further proposed free education to the tertiary education level, no youth in the state wanted to hear any other politicians name anymore. In essence, his achievements before heading to the government house gave him a wide acceptance.

Months into his administration you could see projects springing up everywhere and everyone who saw them would say 'Rochas is working' but none of them knew what was really behind the curtain. Most of the contractors were not being paid, little wonder why the projects were of no set standard. Too many projects were on and no meaningful progress was being made. I will like to chip in here that projects alone don't affect the citizenry directly but programmes do; poverty alleviation schemes, education both formal and informal, job creation, and definitely payment of salaries, wages, allowances, pensions and the likes. Yes, we need projects but they should be geared towards something that can create wealth and better lives.

Also in assuming office he had so much confidence in the ADAPALM which he renamed to Imo Palm Plantation, how it was generating billions monthly. He went on to start a campaign and cited examples of how Asian giants came to take some of our palms to build their nations. Can a nation actually build with just one resource? Singapore had mineral resource but they capitalized in collaboration with other nations in bringing in huge investments in industries, reaching out to nations who can come and leverage on the resilience of their people.

This government owes workers salary from his first administration to the present one. One of his statements in that his powerful inaugural was about former administrations that put money in banks for interest to generate on them while people are not paid.

We are all aware of the bailout by the Federal government for states that owe their workers and I am sure my Imo state was part of this good gesture and spoon feeding. Where then is the money being kept for workers to now go and block the gate of the state assembly because the government plans to privatize government institutions like hospitals while still owing people? The bill for the process has already passed the first reading. At his coming, he came as an advocate for the masses, Mr Governor sir this one is anti-people and wicked because you receive your pay as governor or as a businessman and philanthropist. I am yet to see any effort by your government to create jobs, am not talking about your wife's gestures as a first lady; she has to do it to save her image and yours too.

I also recall the governor emphasizing on jobs and industries for his second administration that I now ask if you didn't create jobs in the first tenure what then did you do? Projects, politics, lawmaking or what please? Is almost 3 months the second administration started and we have not heard that he is on a trip to state in Nigeria or abroad visiting a multinational company in discussion to invest in the state. That should be the body language at this stage, not parading around the President or inaugurating August meetings and New Yam Festivals.

We know your ambitions to be president but will you like to be remembered for nothing at home while you are a king abroad, am sure that *arabako* highlife musician has dwelt enough on coming home to build. This is your opportunity to affect your people positively; you can't be the only saviour for Nigeria, no one person alone saves a Nation. Challenges will always arise and more people will rise to the challenge.

If you surpass Dee Sam's records you will still be remembered beyond Imo State and Nigeria.

13.   INDEPENDENCE EVE |Sept. 30, 1960

The road to self-government and complete freedom from colonial rule has indeed been a hectic one; series of conferences, debates, lobbying, sleepless nights and right now is like that long journey that seemed impossible is drawing to a positive close. A new nation of Africa is about to free itself from the shackles of colonial rule and pave their way to true nationhood.

The years that preceded 1960 witnessed the move of the motion in the house for independence by Anthony Enahoro, followed by consultations by varying parties on whether this nation was ready for self-government. The political climate had 3 political parties- the NCNC in the East, Action Group in the West and the NPC in the North. They were led by three prominent Nigerians; Nnamdi Azikiwe, Obafemi Awolowo, and Ahmadu Bello respectively.

The north was sceptical about independence move considering their level of education and limited personnel to participate in the governance of the prospective new nation. Even though it was agreed that the regions operate a self-government, the north waited until March 1959 for them to adopt this new development.

Due to the relationship, the British have built with the northerners, their size in population, land mass and their number of seats in the house, a northern statesman Tafawa Balewa was picked as the first prime minister of the Emerging Nation. He was later knighted alongside so many other northern leaders.

The four prominent leaders were intelligent and smart but the trust was lacking between them. With a northerner as prime minister, an Easterner the Governor General (a figurehead role), westerners now became the main opposition for the ruling party.

'It is rather unfortunate that we the Yorubas who are well exposed and informed than any other ethnic group have been sidelined as the opposition when we are meant to be leading this nation. We are the light bearers of this nation, we are more learned than all of them and our place at the top must not be denied,' Awo speaking to his tribesmen. So tomorrow we would go and take the third place behind these half-baked tribes that now try to dominate the polity of the new nation we are creating'. He really looked disappointed with the expression of weariness on his face obviously after the work he had done in making sure that tomorrow is realized.

Finally, he added, 'we must not be deterred at this development, in time the Yoruba nation will lead this country and we would show them what we are made of'.

'Let me start by saying that we have achieved a whole lot by having our son here, as the first indigenous governor general, *odighi mfe'*, Festus Okotie Eboh, labour minister speaking to his kinsmen while Zik looked on. Quite alright the north got the lion share but we are better than our Yoruba brothers, *ofe mmanu* will always be what they are. They just make the noise of being educated. The real deal is in securing a good place for oneself.

Zik looked indifferent and reserved and later spoke. 'My fear is in dealing with these northerners, Balewa looks sincere and straightforward but the Sardauna is whom I don't trust. He is like the godfather to the prime minister and will be there to dictate to him. This nation needs people who are sound upstairs to build her in the comity of emerging nations.'

Zik personally had an ambition beyond Nigeria, one that spans across Africa. His kinsmen position is now influencing him to be talking based on ethnic affiliations and sentiments.

The Sardauna's house was filled to the brim with British officials coming in to congratulate him and Balewa on getting the lion's share from this entity called Nigeria.

'Of a truth, I didn't believe we would be able to pull this off in the first place but the queen really had a crucial role to play for us to secure this victory,' the prime minister said with so much excitement and glow radiating from his face.

'I am not surprised myself because we have the population, highest house members, in fact, our limited educated won't have been an obstacle especially when our British friends are here to lend a helping hand'. He laughed hysterically. Tomorrow we go on and lead the country like we have always done. HAPPY INDEPENDENCE EVE, he shouted raising his glass of wine.

14.   RIVERS RERUN: ASSESSING AMAECHI AND WIKE'S LEADERSHIP AND INFLUENCE

The policy, political, socio-economic and economic direction of the present government has made me tread with caution on justifying the present administration or be on the side of those who are out to talk down on them too knowing full well of my stance and allegiance before the general elections last year. From the time of my being political aware till now I have come to understand that despite the drama that ensues from partisanship, support, votes, debates, arguments and twitter fighting; it is still about Nigeria and Nigerians. Not any party, ethnic group but for the good of all. I wish many people will come to realize this anytime they have to make their assertions without having to cut other a fellow Nigeria's neck.

Before I proceed to let out my thoughts on the two people who actually contested the elections in Rivers State; Rotimi Amaechi, a serving Federal Minister and Nyesom Wike, a sitting state governor of the said State (Rivers State) let me also state my description of them before the general elections. For Rotimi Amaechi, I admired him so well especially at during the Governor's Forum saga and the implosion that rocked the PDP under President Jonathan. I loved his courage even though some have said he is arrogant and proud (I am not capable of deciphering some attitudes in a man I have never met). For Governor Nyesom Wike I only saw a man who was bickering because of the support he had from the Presidency and the President's family as well. I saw a man who didn't have decorum in speech, gestures and maybe orientation. I also got to realize that despite that he had some measure of influence in his own constituency. Let me add too that

Duncan Mighty a Nigerian musician mentioned these two people in one of his popular hit songs while acknowledging some Niger Delta strong men.

Now to the business of this piece.

In his book, The Trouble with Nigeria Chinua Achebe in talking about Indiscipline said this, "Leaders are in the language of psychologists, role models. People look up to them and copy their actions, behaviour and even mannerisms. Therefore if a leader lacks discipline the effect is apt to spread automatically down to his followers. He continued; "Power, by giving him (the leader) immunity from common censure, makes the leader the envy of the powerless who will turn him into a role model and imitate his actions of indiscipline. An explosion of such actions occurring all over the place at once brings the whole society under a climate of indiscipline. Third, and fortunately, a leader's undisciplined actions can also incite anger and rebellion."

I guess my story is going too far so I will hit the nail where it can fit.

- There was an outburst of violence in Rivers State re-run elections and both political parties meted out violence on one another.
- Neither Amaechi nor Wike carried out any of those dastardly acts.
- The people who were involved in these acts are all followers of both Wike and Amaechi and all look up to them for guidance and leadership.

Leadership becomes void if there is no followership after the likes of the leader and a leader who cannot assert enough influence over his followers might as well look somewhere else to assert such a leadership or influence. If Amaechi or Wike actually think that their stance on the election or those of their parties means well for the good and entire of Rivers State and those residing there including the murdered corps member then the violence that is raging is really what they want for their people. What kind of influence do they have that motivates youths to carry arms, what kind of influence pushes their followers to take other people's lives, what kind of influence makes people want to share fake result sheets, what kind of influence makes people want to subvert the wishes of the people; whichever way it was supposed to go.

If Amaechi or Wike really think they have influence over the people of River State is it that of promoting peace and harmony or those of inciting rage, hate, indiscipline among those who actually share the same ancestral roots as brothers and sisters and Nigerian citizens then they really need to have a big re-think on what values they are instilling in the younger generation and future leaders.

15.   THE EMOTIONS OF TRIBALISM

Just yesterday our esteem President and Commander-in-Chief appointed a new Group Managing Director of the Nigerian National Petroleum Corporation in the person of Dr Emmanuel Kachikwu and this led to the usual outburst for his various appointments in the new government. Some people have made it their responsibility to prove that President Buhari is only trying to favour northern interests by his body language, even though he has not affirmed this based on utterances. But of course people will always talk and the media must live up to their expectation of news coverage and trend analysis.

It is no news that Nigeria is a volatile state when it comes to issues of religion, tribe and ethnicity and this has to an extent succeeded in taking us away from the main issues of governance and responsive leadership. It is a creation that preceded independence and the British understood that but maybe they felt Africans will always adapt just like whites did in co-habitation.

The new appointment caused a stir within the Igbo folks who were mostly saying they have been marginalized for a long time and that the new GMD is not an Igbo man but just from the South-South region of Delta State. Maybe is the time we revisit the issue of state creation or even demarcate our boundaries based on tribes too.

I don't support marginalization of any group whatsoever and neither will I speak for mediocrity in the name of the federal character or trying to accommodate everyone; that is if over 250 ethnic groups can be accommodated. This tribalism issue is more evident in the older generation and has been found in the younger ones too. But when will all these end? Should we keep waiting until a whole generation has passed then we would have a new one that has no knowledge of its roots and maybe then we would be known as Nigerians?

I love to be called an Igbo man but will not allow it to cause discomfort to another who is not one but is a Nigerian. I will love to celebrate my culture and I know every Yoruba, Hausa, Efik, Ijaw, Ibibio, Jukun, Tiv, Nupe, e.t.c will love to celebrate theirs too. Pardon me if I didn't mention yours because I can't. Our challenge is that we want an attachment to that tribal name in the national politics and public life, why not if we just stick to the states of origin and most importantly as Nigerians.

If at the end tribalism cannot phase out then we must learn to accommodate everyone who feels he is being marginalized. No aspersions! Just let them voice their opinion; they have that right and are equally Nigerians. Zik, Sardauna, Awo, Ojukwu and every one of them understood this and knew the consequence that will be in 50 years time and now they are all cropping up.

It is either we find a way around this, develop a governmental system based on the states as against tribal jingoism we are going to be divided, running in a different direction as against being a one United Nation working towards greatness together.

16.   STATESMEN OVER ELDERSTATESMEN

Firstly, I will like to make reference to a governor who was addressing protesting students and one of the things he said outside the real issue of closing their school was that he should be given respect as an elder. Hellooo! We need to revisit the meaning of elders; we tend to use it for people who have aged in years without making reference to the values they were known for on their way to elderhood.

Yes, elders need respect but when an elder, on the other hand, lacks respect, then something is wrong. These statements; "Respect is reciprocal", "You earn respect", I believe are universally acceptable worldwide and African elders need no special treatment. What elders boast of these days is an experience but of course, "experience can become obsolete". (Pst. Mattew Ashimolowo, ELC, Daystar Christian Centre, 2011). Also before we accord that over-demanding elder seeking respect, we also need to know who and what he was as a young man.

A statesman is one who plays a major role in government and politics for the public good (emphasis on public). We are in dire need of good, responsible, productive, result-oriented leadership in our country. We need people who really can embody what it really means to be a man for the people; those who truly love Nigeria, who can fight colleagues (that are selfish) for the good of the common man. We need intellectuals, creatives, those who are constantly thinking of what to do better for their people or for the office they hold.

In essence, we need a fusion of capacity and integrity to be able to start reaping the benefits of good leadership. That is what we want.

As much as elder statesman is our creation to honour people who have become old/aged whether they pillaged the nation or not; one needs to be a statesman first before advancing to being an elder. Our much coveted National Merit Awards has also in a way shifted to being used to honour those whose journey to old age had no value but in fact depreciated Nigeria and plunged more people into poverty. Honour is still an invaluable commodity and there are many more of such commodities; we need to promote what matters most.

If someone desires to be respected as an elder or statesman or elder statesman, then he needs to work for it. As a statesman you need to be out for the public as you play your governmental role with proofs to show; we need to see that you have made lives better or made our Nigeria better in your own sphere of influence. If you want respect as an elder you need to also earn it and after you have done all else the two can fuse together for you; ELDER STATESMAN.

17.   NATIONAL ORIENTATION AGENCY AND US

It is a well known that the Nigeria of today is in need of real re-orientation and deep change of mindset, values, philosophies, ideologies, thinking patterns, culture, traditions and anything that makes us look less human or belittle us with other western nations or whites generally. Some things we find people indulge in only goes further to justify that even common sense isn't common at all. Our thinking patterns have now been reflected in our doing patterns that even the conscience no longer speaks when it comes to knowing what is right and wrong. I attended an event some time ago and the speaker pointed out one thing that really stuck with me, that we have a culture of disorder as a nation.

A nation where people don't see driving against traffic as wrong, one where a neighbour decides to dump its refuse by the roadside yet the sanitation officials come to lift them for disposal, one where people are ready to sell fake commodity so long as it brings in money for them, they really don't care about if a life is lost through such a commodity. It is in this nation and just this week I saw electric power officials come to change a pole and after doing that they leave the old one broken and into bits and pieces on a link road. It is in this nation that we have road transport and safety officials are more concerned on billing you for not putting on your seat belt but an obstruction on the highway is left to linger for days without attendance. It is in this country that you find people being granted bail for stealing billions yet a handbag thief is beaten, tortured and sentenced to 7 years in prison. It is still in this nation that an Appropriation Bill/Budget is declared missing before review and signing into law. Are we not a joker nation?

That we need a major paradigm shift in our psychic and mind orientation as a nation is highly true especially among the leaders and those in power who can lead the way in crafting a befitting and worthy national ideology for us all. In quoting Chinua Achebe, 'Nigerians are what they are only because their leaders are not what they should be'. This further buttresses the very many definitions of being a leader that has a common bearing on inspiring a group of people towards a particular goal. We need people who already are worthy of character and learning, disposition, decisions and their convictions to show the way for others to follow.

The National Orientation Agency was set up in 2005 with a vision **to develop a Nigerian society that is orderly, responsible and discipline, where citizens demonstrate core values of honesty, hard work and patriotism; where democratic principles and ideals**

are upheld; and where peace and social harmony reign.

The main objectives of the Agency, as provided in Decree 100 of 1993, are to ensure that Government programmes and policies are better understood by the general public. When you visit their website you would agree with me that the vision and mission statements are worthy, concrete, well outlined but as usual implementation and impact is always a challenge in this part of the world. Looking at the main objective it will good to say that the government and her programmes will determine how far they can go in pursuing their vision. If the government of the day does not act in addressing issues that affect the attitude of her people then any agency will be pushing for nothing or pouring water on a rock hoping for a penetration.

Many are glad that the present administration is trying to tackle corruption in high places among public office holders and recovering looted funds. A common man on the street will rejoice over this because they feel these ones are the cause of the hardship in life. Taking a closer look you will agree that the same corruption you have in government is found also in the private sector, informal sectors, on the streets, in buses, parks, churches and mosques, etc. So what the government is doing right now is tackle a small percentage of our problem when a greater war of good and evil is still raging in the society, more vicious and powerful.

As much as this might sound simple to say i.e. a depraved mindset and changing it for good if it is not addressed now and early in this democratic dispensation we might have a problem in our hand because every government will come and do what he thinks is right yet the people are not changed. It is not enough to build projects, schools, hospitals, roads and pipe-borne water; are the people able and equipped morally, intellectually, socially, and otherwise to use all these without abuse. We still see people going to destroy street lights or even put posters in at odd places in the name of adverts, campaigns and church programs.

I will finalize with this, Nigerians will continue behaving the way they think is right thereby creating constant disorder in certain places until some come to tell them it is wrong and why it is so and give them another option of what to do. It is like creating change; you unfreeze what we use to know, put something on the ground i.e. a better option then you freeze that change so there can be continuity when you are gone. The only person that will tell us this is the leadership.

'The trouble with Nigeria is simply and squarely a failure of leadership. There is nothing basically wrong with the Nigerian character. There is nothing wrong with the N Nigeria land or climate or water or air or anything else. The Nigerian problem is the unwillingness or inability of its leaders to rise to the responsibility, to the challenge of personal example which are the hallmarks of true leadership'. Achebe wrote.

18.   SHOULD WE OUTSOURCE NIGERIA?

At the end of a panel discussion on AIT's The Money Show, one of the panellist Mr Patrick Okogie posed the above question on whether we 'should outsource Nigeria' with his argument that Nigeria might be lacking in the true personnel to help us out of our challenges.

Now that got me thinking and I think you should really think about it.

October 1, 1960, is a long time for some people in Nigeria to still be blaming Britain for our woes, to still be complaining about how Nigeria has never been a nation or how unity still remains part of our greatest challenge. No matter the level of the wrong done by Britain, I believe that we had more to gain from them after we were given an opportunity at self-government. As much as Nigeria's configuration is complex and unique, we are not the only nation that is made up of different people with different cultures and ethnic groups.

Nobody will live in denial that our founding fathers didn't know exactly what Nigeria was actually made of or how diverse we were yet; they decided to adopt ethnic partisanship. People say they were smart leaders and personalities but unfortunately, in uniting this country and actually adopting the best political structure, they failed woefully in that and we must admit it.

Admitting that there was a nationhood problem, they still brought in corruption into the equation, very unfortunate for a nation that started a long journey to greatness. *Nigeria's greatness has been on the level of potential since 1960 so we should not even try to*

bring up achievement (individual yes) but collective I disagree vehemently. We have had people who have done Nigeria proud in other nations and across the country but they did that based on their own individual, strong will, efforts and intelligence. Nigeria, as led by her government, is only good at chattering dreams and aspirations of many.

To further complicate issues, a group of young majors decided to quell the corruption and apparent drift in Nigeria and struck, killing many northerners in the process which further escalated the ethnic tension that has existed before independence. From then till 1999 except a brief democratic experience between 1979 and 1983, we kept having one successive coup or the other. The military yet again proved that they didn't have the capacity to do differently from the politicians without even breaking the record of their wrongs.

1999 came, we are still on it, we are still patching, the same people still hold on to power, they bring up their successors with similar mindsets so what we have are the same shades of leaders in different bodies. This is why that question might be pertinent at this time after 56 years of self-government; we have proved that we can't govern ourselves progressively for the good of all.

In case we decide to consider this option, what structures will it take after all many are talking about restructuring?

- We can have a Joseph figure that comes from another country and becomes prime minister over us.
- We could have a Daniel who also was a captive in Babylon come and become the Head of the Presidents or the regional governments we would have.
- We can bring in expatriates like the Ahmadu Bello to do some of the works required to do.
- Or better still we can sign up Nigeria on a website like www.fiverr.com so people can bid or we can get freelancers to do our work for us.

The list can't be limited to the above but the most important question remains if Nigeria has gotten so bad that we actually lack the personnel to deal with the complexity of religion, tribe, institutions, and every challenge we have as Nigeria and Nigerians.

19.   HOW NIGERIA ACCEPTS THE ABNORMAL AS NORMAL

The first thought this title might give you will most likely be "is Nigeria not abnormal or anything close to normal?" As much as we have challenges, laws, rules, principles are broken doesn't mean we should accept it. If you ask me I will say that's the more reasons those in power and their likes will keep acting like actual people in an animal kingdom while we sit and analyze their faults.

I was engaged in a discussion with a colleague about the performance of a former State governor and the issue of looting in government. His view was that he didn't care if politicians looted so long as they work too. Steal but please work, that's his mindset on how politics should be or has become. This is just on a thought or analysis level of two of our challenges; poor governance and corruption. There are a thousand and one of them.

We have a reached a point in national life and journey to nationhood where we accept mediocrity as normal, where we are more permissible in standardized issues, where we praise someone because he did what he was expected and elected to do, where we break laws that are dangerous to us because we feel that the laws are useless and don't matter.

The way we break and allow others break principles and general laws are furiously annoying yet we complain about the recession and other issues that buffet us. Who are we even directing our anger too; the leaders (who are also guilty) or ourselves (who give them credit for performing below average)? It gets even gross and frustrating when you see people justifying a thief in power that is probably causing some of this family members (whether immediate or extended) pain yet he is staunch fan and follower.

We are not even talking about how people sell their souls (not just votes) for a thousand five hundred naira ($4) or indomie noodle (the maiden meal for stomach infrastructure. Thanks to the man from Ekiti; he surely added a vocabulary to our democratic setting.

We are comfortable building roads, boreholes; buying generators and whatever that makes them tick rather than demanding for is ours. The protests we do here don't even get beyond the agbadas of these lootocrats or clueless or deliberate agents of suffering in the midst of plenty. We need to do more and act differently so we don't fall into that book of insanity of Albert Einstein.

There is no need to delve into the many abnormalities we accept from each other and other citizens because you know them and I know them. However, to conclude with what needs to be done, there is a need for us to rise up and call abnormalities by their names, abnormal and treat them like they should be treated. If your device is not working well or your Smartphone you repair or replace them.

There are many things that can replace in this life and one of them in this cases are the elected leaders in power who have the responsibility to give us direction and leadership.

Time has come for us to stop managing abnormalities and treat them like things that act differently against their purpose for being where they are or doing what they should do.

20.   THE PROTEST MARCHES ARE NOT WORKING, CHANGE THE STRATEGY

Nigeria, despite having an unfortunate history of failed leadership, has equally had an equal dose of failed citizenship that has refused to what is expected or workable to hold leaders accountable. We have been adopting the same strategies to justify that we are actually engaging as citizens when they are practically not working. Social media has also been added, protests have been there, blogging to increase journalistic engagement is also there and much; yet the leaders keeping having pot bellies that look healthy in agbada.

The marches from Unity Fountain to the National Assembly or the Presidency have either resulted in nothing or an address from one lying PA or media person or attack by security operatives or simply protesters stand and sit and lie down for hours with no response. The assurances by a

PA are simply a façade to what goes on in the mind of their principals; they are there to do what they are paid to do which is to protect his interests.

However, is this a justifiable reason for us to give up on the country and leave it in the hands of people who lack vision and the necessary skill and know-how to make it work?

The strategies have failed over the years and it is the time we adopt something better. Even as we look forward to the hearing for the Not Too Young to Run bill, I hope that history will be made today, I hope that the NASS will understand that this is history for Africa and the world, I hope that they will usher in this new era of paving the way for young people to participate in the election process beyond voting to the being voted for.

However, if they fail to pass this law; it is expedient that we adopt something better through the ballot that cannot be rigged, through strategies that will keep them at rest, through processes that they cannot ignore or sweep under the carpet. While we remain hopeful, we must also be vigilant not to allow things pass when we can actually do something to bring our hopes into existence.

It is time to take the engagement of our leaders beyond social media, protests, forums, town hall meetings to something more proactive and back-bearing for them.

History is far spent! #NotTooYoungToRun

21.   NIGERIA AS A COMPROMISE ECONOMY

Have you heard of the man called Booker T. Washington; a black African who worked and fought for the liberation of black Africans in the US and freedom every form of racial discrimination. However, he did through the tool of education, enlightenment and acquisition of skills for the people of his race. He was the founder of the Tuskegee Institute and is popularly known for his Compromise Speech in Atlanta; where he defiled every notion of simply speaking for black freedom but instead pushed that blacks attained relevance by building capacity and skills. It is a great speech everyone needs to have.

This piece is not the kind of compromise speech he offered on that day but focuses on the anomaly in Nigeria that has eaten deep into the fabric of our national life, through the eroding of good values, coupled with bad governance in government and a hope lost in the rich and leaders of our land.

To compromise means to renege on what you stand for, to do the opposite of what is expected, to default on your integrity, to go back on your word, to change the course of action and more. All these can be done either for good or bad, to steal, to kill, to dupe, to rob and more. It is equally done to reach a consensus, to let the other person have their way and more. For the case of Nigeria being a compromise nation, I will be discussing how people get what is good by giving what is bad in return. Don't think too much, because there are many things to consider here.

Mind you, not everyone sets out to compromise or do what is bad to get what is good. I can remember those in school while we were preparing for SSCE when someone said that he will use God, his head and chokes (malpractice) to pass the exams. Can you imagine? What that experience taught me was that on our own we can limit God or simply show that we don't trust if we have to have plan Bs and support for Him. That's another day's story.

Don't be offended if any of the scenarios apply to you but it is the truth and truths are meant to be told and equally heard.

- We have been become largely a nation where people believe in making money dubiously and call it being smart or smart work; I am sorry but I believe in working hard with your brains not playing pranks.

- Nigeria has degenerated so bad where people tell you that the earn N,40,000 monthly but are able to pay rents of N500,000 and every other person see it as normal.

- We are talking about corruption and stealing in high places yet we refuse to focus on the corruption that happens in the lower and unseen places. How people, for instance, know that a big man is a looter of the treasury yet the stay put as foot soldiers because bills are being paid (not minding it is a loot).

- Have you been on Instagram to see posts of young ladies who flout their bodies proudly, are bloggers without any domain name or website, reveal or cleavages you can imagine and of course leaving fabulously well. Quick add: the looters above pay most of those bills.

- We also have a situation where young ladies give bodies for a job that pays N70, 000 (just to get Appointment letters) and you and can imagine what happens when the fools (employers) feels he needs to taste of what he had when he offered her the job.

- Let me add on a general note that money + the love of it and the way it is gotten in this country in many ways justifies the Bible as the root of all evil. The compromises are not surprising but the scene and situations are heart-wrenching.

In conclusion of my postulations (that might have made me your enemy right), let me add that most people that are engaged in all these, annoyingly give credit to God or thank Him for blessing them. Why are we making this Great and Mighty God look petty when He is dignified in every ramification?

Why then are we religious, why do we praise and pray? Let me a shock you!

Nigeria as a religious nation has done little with the substance that is in God while focusing on religiosity without value or substance that reflects in our daily life or work. How do you explain that someone is religious yet at work, he/she is lackadaisical to work?

We break many principles to take hold of the blessings of others. We need help!

22.   WHY WE NEED A READING REVOLUTION

In a knowledge economy like the 21st century, what we have is a deluge of ideas that are gotten so long as your mind is awake, there is air, if you experience life more then you will have more than enough of them. Ideas are ruling the world, they have become really marketable, they are capital assets of the mind, can be converted from just thoughts to value and real cash. However, this does not happen overnight, there are processes, phases and much more if you are to get technical and speak in economic terms.

An idea remains an idea if it cannot be communicated in a manner that anyone can grab what you want to achieve with it or the problem you solving with your product. Communication and articulation skill is key for the conveyance of thoughts and ideas as they are crystallized in your mind. There is a marked difference between one who can articulate thoughts and those who can't. Clear and marked difference!

The easiest and cheapest way to learn self-expression is to read, read and read wide as possible. Reading is not just a way of downloading words from an author into your being; there are a lot more things that happen by having books embedded in your mind.

According to **Oscar Wilde**, "It is what you read when you don't have to that determines what you will be when you can't help it."

- Reading can serve as a way of escape from the frustrations of the world around you. Depending on what type of pictures that are created by the book, you can experience something different from what pertains to you.

- There are people who have not had the opportunity to travel wide or leave the shores of their country; through reading they can scale mountains, pass seas and oceans to understand what really happens in the world beyond their borders.

- Through reading, you can connect to the mind and the very being of the author, you are able to know the man/woman, you can access their secrets to an extent and in some cases, you experience transference of grace.

- The many details of success in life, inventions, innovations, ideas, creativity are embedded in words. If you don't sit down and read the details of a headline or title, you will only gain access to the wordings of the headline and its meaning.

- No nation can go beyond their extent and level of research and development which require a lot of studies, research, searches, data gathering, analysis and a complete understanding of whatever you read.

- There is a secret I discovered about reading a book; you don't just limit yourself to the words contained in the book. There is need to think, look, and discover beyond what the words say. Behind every letter of a word, there is more and greater meaning of what the author is saying.

- Anyone who can discover details in many words can discover anything and it can help your observation and attention to details.

"A great book should leave you with many experiences, and slightly exhausted at the end. You live several lives while reading.'

— ***William Styron, Conversations with William Styron***

- Reading, of course, is the easiest way to learn to write and write well. There is nothing to write if you don't read. The icon of writing Stephen King puts it this way, ***if you don't have time to read, you don't have the time (or the tools) to write. Simple as that.***

- Books, of course, help to preserve civilization, they preserve culture, a nation that lacks writers (who are readers) and chroniclers of their history will in no time find their culture exterminate without noticing it.

"You don't have to burn books to destroy a culture. Just get people to stop reading them."

— **Ray Bradbury**

23.   NIGERIA: ANOTHER ELECTION YEAR WITHOUT DEMOGRAPHIC DATA

Elections, like anywhere in the world is characterized by political leaders and politicians making promises upon promises, giving hope that cannot be verified or seen as being possible and Nigeria and Africa are no different. While we are still years behind other nations that are already manufacturing flying self-driving taxis, cars and vehicles that run on clean energy like electricity, our national, citizen, the social and political atmosphere are saddening, to say the least. The country is speedily approaching another election year and politicians will start giving us hope that are largely false yet we have no real information on the population of people that make up our country.

How does a leader in politics or a President make promises to a nation he/she does not understand know or understand the population of their people? The last population census was in 2006 and it is expected that such exercise is done every ten years worldwide. Each time Nigeria's population is made reference to people are quick to describe us as over 180 million people and many know that the truth in this needs some questioning. The demographic data of any country is the most important data there is to nation building; it should be the determinant for almost every key decision in governance.

I will be sharing with you on why we need to understand our national demographic data and why any decision of those in power will either be useless, less impactful or fraudulent with knowing our numbers.

The National Budget

This is the next most important legal document of government after the national constitution. It details the various programs of government, it is a to-do list for governance, and it is the working document to understand the priorities of any government. The national budget is the true reflection of a government's ideas in figures, numbers, projects and programs. A budget, therefore, is what will determine the impact of a government on her people and there is no way to have a comprehensive impact on this document without a detailed understanding of your people. The drafting of the budget should be done based on the demographic distribution of citizens, the needs of the people must be understood, what is lacking in particular with either thousand or million people must be understood before it will be included in the national budget. Any budget that is drafted without a real data, figures and understanding of the people is simply a document to allocate money, not for good governance.

The budget is a general overview of government's programs but the next points will give a detailed application of population demography in governance.

National Housing

Housing is a major need of man and every government is expected to make provisions for their people. We have housing policies that seek to build 10,000 housing units for workers in government or otherwise. There is no way housing allocations can be made for a particular location without knowing the population of such places. Provision of housing equally comes with providing social amenities like schools, hospitals and other services that human beings need to live decently. There are dire situations where many people live in a particular environment or house way above the required standard that is conducive for habitation and comfort.

See below the World Health Organization standard for living spaces (in square metres) against a number of the persons.

Area (in sq. metres)	No. of Persons
11 or more	2 persons
9 to 10	1.5 persons
7 to 9	1 person
5 to 7	0.5 persons
Under 5	Nil

Note: Babies under 12 months are not counted and for children between 1 to 10 years, they are counted as half a unit. (WHO)

Different countries used various standards, some are stricter than others but the essence of this is that when providing housing for citizens it is important to know their demographic data. The population of children and adults is important to determine the allocation and eventual construction.

Transportation System

I will make this as simple as possible with the daily experience of everyone. Transportation system involves the following; the number of road users, the location of residence, size of roads and construction quality. If you are living in an estate where you have to experience delayed traffic movement because of the large influx of people then there is a problem in the planning of such transport system. If some roads get congested in the mornings or evening, it means that enough efforts were not made to understand the direction of traffic flow where people are living and where they work, the population and number of people that have cars. This area and other areas involve the analyses of population data using various parameters of either age, religion, sex, income level, occupation and others that might have an effect on traffic movement.

Power Generation

Though our power generation issue needs to be fixed by the law that makes provision for the national grid, we still need to address how demographic data can play a role in it. The nature of sharing power among various locations due to voltage level is really embarrassing. Power usage is dependent on the population and the extent of usage by each household or corporate entity. If a particular Megawatt of power is to be transmitted to a particular location, then their usage level needs to be verified and allowances made for any form of overshoot for such places. For instance, a particular place in Lekki, Lagos or Maitama, Abuja needs 500 MW after checking every building then the power generation company can make it 700MW should any household buy more electrical appliances that will take up more power.

Other Social Amenities

We have situations where a doctor is allocated to about 500 patients, a teacher to about 200 students, classrooms too small for students to get a seat for lectures, hospital spaces and beds not being enough for the sick, the police force or military not populated enough to safeguard citizens and many areas that get shortchanged due to lack of population data.

On what basis will the next round of politicians convince on what they intend to do for us in Nigeria when we don't know the actual population of Nigerians and foreign residents. We have not even started talking about those in the diaspora and the ones that get unfortunate of being deported from countries where they are. The importance of demographic data cannot be overemphasized, they are the foundation of any development plan, national plans, regional and state plans.

With such data, we are able to plan for the future, make plans and secure the generation yet unborn.

24.   THE HALLMARK OF LEADERSHIP

At the end of his tenure and eventual death as president Abraham Lincoln was remembered as a man who saved the union through a Civil War, abolished slavery and signed the Emancipation Proclamation. Sir Winston Churchill today is remembered for leading Britain into

World War and inspiring a generation of Britons that they could confront the enemy in the seas, on land, mountains and valleys. Ronald Reagan is remembered as one who saved America from the Great Depression. Bill Clinton ushered in America into new levels of prosperity leading up to the 21st century.

Lee Kuan Yew will be remembered until the end of times as the leader that worked for the transcendence of Singapore from a Third World to a First World Nation. Back home in Africa Nelson Mandela will long remain in the heart of South Africans as the father of modern democracy and a symbol of reconciliation among white and black South Africans. There are many outstanding leaders the world has produced in many nations and each one has their way of celebrating theirs but one thing in common; their achievements when in power speak volumes more after the exit power.

A wise man once said every leader thinks of the next generation and I will add that every leader also thinks of his life after parading the corridors of power. What is next for him and how will the world or people he served to treat him or regard him as? The impact you make as a leader might not hold sway or mean much until after you have vacated office. It is such an irony especially for someone who has attained the highest office in his country like being President; he will need to ask himself some sincere but tough questions. Bill Clinton I hear was given 10 million dollars to write his autobiography and he made more money sharing his experience as President through public speaking.

Here in Nigeria our immediate past President earned his place in Africa for a smooth transition of power to another democratically elected President saving us from the predictions of doom that filled 2015 general elections. He will be long remembered. The greatest mistake anyone will make in life is to think that ascension to power means the peak of it all for you. In fact, it is an opportunity for you to chart your future after that office either for good or bad.

In as much as you will enjoy the attention and attractions of that office, your real worthy attraction will be decided when at the end of it all you are appraised by the history of your actions, inaction, decisions and whatever that constituted your leadership. In fact, you will live to answer even for the actions of those you appointed as subordinates or your men.

The hallmark of your leadership is not while you are in power but when you are out of power because then you, your subjects, history and the public will judge the success of whatever you did in power. Your reward will be to know that your achievements will stand the test of time.

25.   DUE PROCESS AND THE URGENCY OF NOW

The level we find ourselves after over 50 years of independence, the level of corruption over the years, the impunity of office holders, poverty, hunger, and deprivation has created a sort of siege mentality on the land. It is such that everyone is eager to achieve and make ends meet through the newly found system of Africapitalism and a free market enterprise. This siege mentality sparked up revolutions that were experienced in Northern Africa. This awakening and frustrations of tyrants and impunity in the system led to such agitations and it reached the shores of West Africa when Nigeria nearly degenerated into such situations.

For many in Nigeria especially young people it was periodic of political awakening and consciousness, social media became a tool of engagements and even controversies. It kind of made the internet space more interesting as Nigerians will always make a joke of little and serious issues. Events that followed had a proliferation of politically aware and conscious people; both naïve and the ones who know the ropes, literate and illiterate. It somewhat baffling and exciting when you see a roadside seller or peddler analyze the Commander-in-Chief and the kind of person he is even more than he knows himself.

That is the Nigeria we have now; of people with what Nuhu Ribadu called positive anger in one of his presentation at TED Talks. Now to the crust of the matter.

Democracy is well known for institutions and various levels of bureaucracy because it should be based on rule of law. So there is a rule guided by law that must be followed. I personally believe that rules can change but laws are like the heavens they can never change. As much as our constitution is sacrosanct when it comes to all issues

Nigerian, the rules of engagement of such laws can change so that other things can fall into place. Who says the days for signing a bill into law must be done after a certain period or that an agreement to establish industries by a foreign company must go through the strenuous bureaucratic processes that characterize the corridors of power.

To borrow the mantra of the ruling party in Nigeria (All Progressives Congress), there is an urgent need for change in the land. People want to be proud locally not just while in a foreign land. Rather than slow down the pace of achieving a Nigeria and prolonged suffering we desire forward movement. If the budget is missing the waste no time responding do media hype and analyses, produce another so long as it is not breaking any law.

We need to trim down various bureaucratic levels that might limit the passage of key decisions that will impact lives and make Nigerians feel better. The public and civil servants should be made to understand that now is not the time for cooling off and gradualism. Africa is already 50 years backwards; those we started the race with are leading the world and we can't afford to mortgage another

50 because we want to obey the tenets of democracy that are subject to change and flexibility.

Some 53 years ago at the façade of Lincoln Memorial in Washington D.C, Dr Martin Luther King Jr in declaring his dream he said;

"We have also come to this hallowed spot to remind America of the fierce urgency of now. This is no time to engage in the luxury of cooling off or take the tranquillizing drug of gradualism. Now is the time to make real the promises of democracy; now is the time to rise from the dark and desolate valley of segregation to the sunlit path of racial justice; now is the time to lift our nation from the quick sands of racial injustice to the solid rock of brotherhood; now is the time to make justice a reality for all of God's children. It would be fatal for the nation to overlook the urgency of the moment."

Nigeria and Africa need such urgency!

26.   NIGERIA: A HISTORY OF REPEAT

'Our enemies are the political profiteers, the swindlers, the men in high and low places, that seek bribes and demand 10 percent; those that seek to keep the country divided permanently so that they can remain in office as ministers or VIP's at least, the tribalists, the nepotists, those that make the country look big for nothing before international circles, those that have corrupted our society and put the Nigerians political calendar back by the words and deeds.'

The above statement was made on January 15, 1966, by a young man whose discourse and the name has sparked up a lot of controversies regarding that particular day. It is difficult to say it is a day that will live in infamy; either way for the lives lost that day it can be regarded as one but for the purpose of the exercise which some see as a near revolution for our country Major Chukwuma Kaduna Nzeogwu actions and those of his colleagues that day revealed what many turned a blind eye to about our realities as a country. Even though he was not the mastermind of the coup (which was led by Major Emmanuel Ifeajuna), the success of his command in northern Nigeria made it seem like he was the leader of the coup plotters.

The events of that day altered the course of history and rather than achieve its purpose as outlined in the above quote, it deepened the mess we found ourselves in. I don't know if there is a justification for taking another's life in order to perpetuate their goal of ridding Nigeria of corrupt politicians, nepotists, tribalists, bribe givers and takers; but one thing is sure we lost some great Nigerians that day, unfortunately, they were mostly of the northern stock.

So these men at that time recognized that the political class was destroying the fate of a new nation that the whole world looked up to in leading the black race and continent. Those who take bribes and demand for a percentage when they have to help you process a procurement or contract document. The ones that insist you must empty your pockets for them if you don't want your file to be sent to archives before its time. These are the tax collectors of civil and public service.

He further went to describe that they are people in high and low places. I sure like this and really hope President Buhari will take cognizance of this one. Corruption and issuance of bribes are not found in high places alone but also found more in low places. The private sectors, informal economy, on the streets, motor parks, small businesses, schools, churches, organizations that don't even have to trifle with government funds yet they are destroying the fabric of our macro and micro-economy.

We also have those who want the country divided because they are in one way or the other profiting from our disunity. Those who want the insurgents to keep razing our towns and villages because they are beneficiaries of monies meant to quell such attacks. They want to remain in power for what it offers them rather what they have to offer the country.

Then to those who tend to make the country look big to the international community. Hypocrites who only are concerned about telling lies of having the largest economy yet poverty level is at over 70 % of the entire population. Those who will not tell the world the truth about the realities on the ground and what faces us as a nation and what that common man on the street is going through in order to find something to eat or a place to lay his head on.

Chukwuma was by nature and upbringing, incapable of planning, let alone executing a coup d'état designed to deliberately suppress one tribe politically and elevate another. But the exceptions of their plans in the South were susceptible to such an interpretation. He was unhappy about it. He felt disappointed, almost betrayed. There was no intention on Chukwuma's part, to collude or conspire with Ibo officers in the army and with Ibo politicians and academics, to lead a coup for the purpose of ensuring the political leadership of Nigeria by Ibos. No doubt, Ibos and non-Ibos gave a sigh of relief when the coup took place. However, some sections of the Nigerian society saw the coup as a monumental and wholesale Ibo plot to establish Ibo political ascendancy, supremacy and domination.

-Olusegun Obasanjo, in Nzeogwu.

The above assertion by the author remains a major issue of discourse, arguments and counter-arguments till date; whether the events of January 15, 1966, was aimed at perpetuating Ibo dominance in the Nigerian Army and the political space. This same feeling led to the second coup in July targeted at mainly Ibos. This and subsequent events degenerated into a full-blown war between Federal

Government of Nigeria and the then secessionist Eastern Nigeria.

Rather than just repeating the mistakes of history in Nigeria we have made history to live amongst us and this keeps drawing us back even when it seems we have moved forward considerably. The Nigeria of 1960-70 still very much lives with us talk more of the years after.

No nation will ever develop beyond her abilities to work together as one despite their disparities of tribe, race, religion and ethnic groups. The visions are different. Everyone is seeking a stake for his kinsman. In fact, the situation has degenerated to each one now concerned about the national cake and how he can partake of it. It is highly unfortunate.

As Achebe will always insist, our challenge has been the problem of leadership and I agree with him; why? It is only a purposeful and responsible leadership that can give a people direction, purpose, vision, a collective goal and break the barriers and sentiments that have lingered on and on. The distrust is highly polarized, politically, socially, ethnically, tribally, religiously and what have you.

We need a government that will make us understand the danger of our actions and inaction as a people and how it is impeding our growth and development. We need a Nigerian Dream that can resonate with everyone's aspiration and dream. A dream that every child will be made to learn about. A dream that every business owner can run with and imbibe in their companies. A dream that every public servant will be zealous to defend with whatsoever he/she holds dear. A dream that the world will see, hear, feel and reckon with this African giant.

What is our Nigerian Dream?

27.   DO SOLDIERS MAKE BETTER LEADERS; AND WHY?

There is a universal trend of having former military get involved in politics or business to the point of making CEOs and even Presidents and Heads of State under a democratic dispensation. Many nations have had it this way; from the United States to Britain to Rwanda and

Nigeria. There is a George Washington, John F. Kennedy, Paul Kagame, Olusegun Obasanjo, etc.

Many believe that they actually make better leaders and in this piece, I will highlight why and how their military leadership experience helps them in government or business.

Training and Experience that that get in wartime and as soldiers. They tend to get better training than those in other sectors that require leadership because military training is regimented, rigorous, progressive (improvement is monitored based on the practical capacity of soldiers), time-consuming and equally expensive. Wartime experience of a military helps them in better decision making. A general in the theatre of war and in harm's way must take a decision that will either kill his men or himself. Decision making is key to any leadership and when done under pressure and danger, there can be no better experience or exposure.

The sense of duty to serve, self-sacrifice (including paying the ultimate price) and all these are backed up by an oath. Most people who find themselves in the military do so out of sheer will to serve. Many even live the easy life of other jobs and sectors because they want to serve their country neglecting the dangers in wartime.

The selflessness that comes with being exposed to danger is incomparable. When a General prefers putting himself in danger as against exposing his men, they will follow and fight willingly. Even the rewards that are transactional mean nothing anymore to them because such reward like money, housing will only benefit family since they can lose their lives in battle.

The military experience offers one many side to leadership and works ethics physically, intellectually and otherwise. Courage, discipline, self-control, restraints, obedience to authority, agility and much more help both in the business circle and politics.

Credit: ***Harvard Business Review***

## 28.	BUHARI AS A SOCIALIST

In my economics class as a secondary (high) school student, I was taught that Nigeria has a mixed market system that is a mix of socialism and capitalism but more of free enterprise. Many years after I learnt about economic systems all I still see prevailing in the land is a high level of capitalism that has pitched the rich against the poor. That might be some bad news though but the good news is this.

This has created a kind of entrepreneurial spirit in many people who now think everything is possible in business by applying the many principles others have used. This is applicable to all spheres of businesses, scale, size and approach to them. A fish seller and garri seller are all capitalists in their own right. They are creating wealth for themselves, working for themselves, in charge of their time, not having to answer to an overbearing boss, can go on vacation like our President just did and many pecks and definitely challenges of running a business.

In essence, Nigeria has become more of a free market churning out different shades of capitalists but despite all these and the challenge of doing business under harsh conditions, many are still languishing in poverty and dire need of minimum basic amenities like good water, shelter, clothing, healthcare, education, etc. All these have become more of a privilege when we understand that it should be a right of every citizen.

The argument that the challenge of Nigeria has always been a failure of leadership can never be wrong for all the right reasons. Our governments have become dormant and more like only the regulators of the economy when in actual sense they should play key roles of building government-owned businesses run by citizens. This will be way beyond the civil service of laxity and be laid back while the system rots.

While on the campaign trail, President Buhari promised welfare programs for the unemployed and vulnerable in the society and he has made good this promise by providing 500 billion naira in the controversial 2016 budget. That's more like a socialist style even though the procedures have not been enumerated for us to know the direction it will go. Socialism has always been a situation where the government takes charge of the resources of the state and as the manager of it.

Rather than just pay a monthly wage of ₦5, 000 to unemployed graduates as part of the welfare program there should be an effective way that will make such fund go a long way for the beneficiaries. A distinction should be made between those already educated but unemployed and those who don't have the privilege of being in school who are mostly unskilled jobs that benefit little. For instance the hawkers on the street, market sellers of consumer goods, cleaners, etc.

These ones will rather spend the money on meeting short-term needs and even when they want to use it to make more money the skill to channel it into most likely won't be there.

The program can take the form of taking these young men and women off the streets, trained them on skills that can actually help them set up a business. They need to be made to learn how to add value by making themselves valuable through various skill acquisition programs.

We are talking about industrialization and mining in the near future after the oil market shake-up around the world. This is the time to also train these unskilled workers on handling machines or factory equipment while we make plans to set the agenda going. It is unfortunate to say that

Africa, as it were, didn't go through the complete cycle of nation-building and wealth creation. The world is talking about a knowledge economy and information age that was preceded by manufacturing and use of heavy equipment when in actual sense it is the western world that has evolved and produced products that can reflect such a transition. Nigeria or Africa can't boast of much heavy equipment produced here and it has nothing to do with raw materials being present; we just haven't explored that age-long word "potential".

We have been in the potential stage for too long and it is high time we activated the kinetic aspect and move our nation forward. Rather than to continue running a system that engenders more capitalists, neglecting the poor, creates enmity between the poor and rich maybe it is time to carry the vulnerable along with such welfare programs.

What these uneducated ones lack is knowledge, maybe not just theoretical knowledge but more application of their physical strength in making money, why not engage them in something more worthwhile that requires the intellect and the physical strength to match with like industry-related activities.

29. POLITICS BEREFT OF IDEOLOGIES

The purpose of this piece is not to denigrate what has been achieved in terms of political system, arrangement or our democracy but to state the obvious to those who can see and how it is bad for a young Nation and what best we can work things out.

Every human endeavour whether secular or religious or otherwise should have a purpose, a reason for existence and the force driving it. Nobody sets up anything without having a reason for doing so.

Politics alone is a huge enterprise that rules, runs, have spoilt, uplifted and shaped the world we live in. It is one institution that affects the whole world and her systems. It is the leading leader of all institutions. As a business, family, NGO, company, organization, you subscribe to the leadership of either your President, Head of State, Governor and everyone who plays this game (politics).

Looking at American politics where you have two major political parties- Democrats and Republicans or Liberals and Conservatives. Liberals for those who believe in civil rights, government participation, progressives in nature and the social and economic good, while conservatives for the ones that believe in the minimal participation of government, support private enterprise and a conservative governance style. In the context of America, of course, there are those who are mixed in their own ideologies.

Coming to my beloved country Nigeria, at present we have two major political parties because they have the number, influence, clout, crème de la crème and the big wigs in the society. I just gave you a reason why they are the two major. This is asides the over 20 more political parties we have all across the country.

Now these parties, two major ones inclusive when they discuss politics, democracy and governance, what we hear are projects, programs and what they will do when in office. Everybody knows that as a government you must work for your people, but does spending money have to be the only reason why a party wants to be in government.

I don't think so!

Ideologies, values, principles are what should guide every party, members and their faithful. Is like having a thought pattern that drives you and principles that guides someone. When a party is based on ideologies and philosophies, they would base their action and inactions on these. Every decision made will only be propelled by the values they have stood for over time. Partisanship shouldn't be about canvassing for votes based on promises, what you will do and have done because anyone can give a directive to spend money on projects.

On the other way, round philosophies make you tackle issues that build and make democracy work. You can come out and discuss intelligently on issues that directly affect the economy, lives and the people you are leading. You can build projects yet the people are not any better. Values are there not just to guide but to help one create ideas and execute ideas based on them. A perverted value will create a perverted idea so a noble value will create a noble idea.

Another election year is around the corner in my Nation and it is pertinent for politicians to start discussing the real issues that nations are built on- rule of law, economy, business, welfare, fiscal policy, foreign policy, security, unemployment, job creation, industrialization, empowerment, etc. We should let them debate issues of governance and we don't want to hear 'we would pump in more money', obviously you will need more money to run the country. Tell us strategies, well laid out plans, make us understand how well you know the challenges we now face and other global challenges facing the world.

We should not be called the giant of Africa for just discussing meagre issues that don't count much. We should be known for intelligent, rational, analytical and constructive reasoning. Nigeria and Africa have advanced well enough for shallow minded issues.

30.   LEADERSHIP: BOYCOTTING BUREAUCRACY

Before I delve into this seemingly self-explanatory topic let me share an experience with you on my Christmas journey from Port Harcourt to Owerri, both capital cities of Rivers and Imo states, Nigeria respectively. Due to limited flights in Owerri, I had to go through Port Harcourt and unfortunately, the airport renovation that was started is far from being completed. Passengers literally struggle to get their luggage under a canopy both domestic and international flights alike.

Now to my near frustration on that journey. The road that leads from the airport all the way to Owerri as it is has been segmented into what you can call the proofs of responsible leadership and irresponsible leadership. It is a trunk A (federal road) so it is expected that the central government will take responsibility for it. The proof of responsible leadership of the road spans from Port Harcourt all the way to the boundary line of the two states (Rivers and Imo); on record, it was constructed by the State government of former governor Chibuike Amaechi.

The other stretch was started by the Federal government but put on hold and the State government of Imo still believes that the central government saddled with many infrastructural projects will come and salvage the situation and save us from such shame.

Leadership is primarily about taking responsibility in making things happen even if it means breaking the rules of success but not the law. The reason for bureaucracy is so people will not break the law of due process. Bureaucracy is not supposed to make a government irresponsible, negligent or laid back in the name of laws, jurisdiction, and what have you. If a road is a trunk A road and you build it as state government, people won't be concerned about your jurisdiction but on the fact that you stood up to make life easier for them.

As much as you have to make things happen as a leader, they shouldn't be liabilities or a burden on your people. As much as capital projects look more like investments over time they can become huge liabilities especially when we have a bad culture of maintenance.

And when can a leadership decision become a burden?

A number of factors can contribute to this but one, in particular, is a misplacement of priorities, taking the wrong decisions or the right decisions at the wrong time. You can be making plans without considering the implications with the parameters of time, efforts, money, value and the desired effects. It is unfortunate that budget presentation or documents are not placed side by side with the manifesto of government. Maybe today they are. As much as we want to pay salaries and so forth, feasibility checks and analysis are equally important because that will determine if a fiscal year can be tagged as successful or a failure or just one of those years of economic downturn.

Failure starts with any leadership or person who knows only to pass the buck to another.

31.   ...IN NEED OF A MAN

It is often said that a tree cannot make a forest but we also forget that it is when that tree sheds some of its fruits and seeds, would other similar trees spring up. If it is a good tree then it would replicate its nature in other trees that are growing and upcoming. Likes the say begets likes i.e. there won't be any slight struggle to reproduce others; it will just have to happen naturally.

Our greatest need right now as a Nation is that man whose track records, integrity and love for mankind will command a natural following. A man whom the opportunists will love to follow. A fisher and a maker of men, who would bring everyone along on the path we need to go.

The major task of this man would be to chart a course for our future; one that everyone would adhere to irrespective of ethnicity, gender, religion or ideologies. A man that breaks every myth that has held us bound for too long- of corruption, tribalism, nepotism, selfishness, negligence and hypocrisy. A man that can be the face of a New Nigeria, whom everyone would be glad and willing to run after.

A leader, selfless personality, a lover of people, one who has the heart to see others move forward, who can pay any price for the good of our Nation. A man who can travail for this Nation in prayers is who God and the people of this country are looking for; who will strain himself that our Nation might live in Unity and Faith, Peace and Progress.

One who dares and has the courage to do justice irrespective of who is involved; who puts the greater good above special interests. A leader who would be courageous to take on the enemies of our Nation in battle. This man will be glad and willing to identify with anyone irrespective of their class, origin, state, tribe/ethnicity, background and ideologies.

We need a man who will give us a Nigerian Dream, inspire us and give us a good reason to pursue it against tribal and party lines.

But who will this man be?

32.   IGBO: THE NEW IDENTITY

There is a sort of siege mentality which our people have acquired as result of the end of the war. I believe this must cease. I believe our people must face the fact that the war is ended, they must feel free to partake, to serve, to benefit from Nigeria. They should have no inhibitions about being Nigerian. They should have no complexes.

- Chukuemeka O. Ojukwu

Before the Civil War (Nigeria-Biafra) which pitched the Ibo people of the then Eastern Nigeria against the Federal side of Nigeria, Ibos were seen as a people highly progressive and most times intimidating. They were found in almost every state of the federation; as traders, businessmen and women, technocrats, public servants, national leaders, etc. They had that attitude for survival and eventually thriving optimally.

In essence, in public and national life, these people were in the forefront in pre-war Nigeria.

Now the war is over 45 years after and there is still that notion that they are still marginalized. Some people might disagree, while some others will affirm this situation.

Marginalization I will say is relative and can come in various shades; exclusion from politics, public service and appointments, verbal attacks, nepotism, etc. These are common in a multi-ethnic and lingual society like ours.

Also, I have noticed that Ibos are mostly involved in local politics that involve their own people e.g. governors, House of Representatives members, Senators, LG chairmen, State House of Assembly members, and any position that demands compulsory participation by Ibos. In other positions like the Presidency and National Assembly leadership, key appointments, they are seen as featherweights.

The businessmen and women among them are either out of the radar of the press or just choose not to be recognized by many. It is like having a phobia for the press and media.

Going further, the ones in the entertainment industry just choose to make their movies, get paid and live a life away from the paparazzi. You can take a mind survey if you wish to. The artists too are more business inclined than being in media controversies.

This type of marginalization might be by choice caused by a form of stereotype by other ethnic groups who are quick to judge anything Igbo. The thought of an Igbo president is like rewriting Nigeria's story.

Whichever the case, there can never be any ethnic nationality as progressive as Ibos, their business sense and wealth creation instinct might be what Nigeria needs to meet up with challenges of nation-building and revenue generation.

The Ibos are more or less the type of people whose desire is mainly to dominate everybody. If they go to a village, to a town, they want to monopolize everything in that area...

-Sir Ahmadu Bello

33.   MONEY: LESSONS FROM MY FATHER

The lessons of great men and women are incomplete without giving credence to their attachments to the parents; some fathers, other their mothers and some others their grandparents. No matter the level of education or studies you attain, lessons are drawn by constant contact under the same roof remains invaluable. They remain with you for as long as choose to apply them.

Barack Obama told us about Dreams from his Father, David Oyedepo talks about great tutelage under his grandmother, Tunde Bakare in an interview with the Interview magazine talks about his plans to write a book;

Lessons my Mother Taught me. There are many others as well.

Personally, I have learnt a lot from my father. Above all else, I can only describe him as one who has a good heart for people. He is a man of empathy. I am yet to find anyone as selfless as he is and with the kind of heart he has for the less privileged in the society. Even a part of his business was run just to help those in our local community especially the young ones.

There is a popular saying that people don't care how much you know until they know how much you care. By how much you know this can be your education, status in the society, your opinion on issues, likes and dislikes and whatever you hold dear. Caring, on the other hand, most times is validated by how liberal you are with people especially economically (money). What drives people these days is what they can lay their hands on, money-wise and making a living, so when you prove that you can meet such a need partially and at some instances, they will be willing to do anything for you.

In my father's words, " in your dealings with people, learn to appreciate them with money no matter how small, that will make them be willing to go the extra mile for you". These words help guide me in impacting lives the little way I can and my little life has been characterized by people who are need of this thing that makes the world go round; money!

I know his mechanics that he uses will always leave whatever they are doing to attend to him/me whenever he calls on them, not because of what they will after their work alone but also due to how he has treated them in the past. Giving them a little above what they should collect normally goes a long way in winning them over. An extra 500 naira ($2.50) might be what you will need to get preferential treatment from them no matter who else might be involved unless the other person does same.

We should understand that money actually makes the world go round and it is he who is liberal with it that has the power to continue spinning the world. A good client can never be compared to a difficult who thinks he is doing you a favour by paying for a service you are offering. You don't need to have a registered foundation in your name to bless people with your wealth; if you have one good enough.

A tip to show some appreciation of a good deed is worth it (not giving money to buy favours; that's a bribe).

When you realize that money actually makes the world go round and how to use for your own influence by being liberal with it, then your relationships with people that come into your life will be a whole easier, stress-free and for your own benefit. You sow a seed of appreciation through it, you reap better services (treatment) from people.

34.   THE TREND OF MODERN DAY MATCH-MAKING

In quoting Pro. 18:22 in one of his messages to Covenant University graduating students, Dr David Oyedepo had this to say; he who finds a wife (not who they find a wife for) findeth a good thing and obtains favour from the Lord. This seems difficult to comprehend or even analyze the truth embedded in this short scripture, but looking at it from the *finding* perspective it sounds like common sense to me. Why may you ask? Choosing a wife that will please your every being and makes you tap into the favour that marriage carries should be a personal choice for the man. You choose who pleases your heart. If otherwise happens then you would be trading your happiness for the reason of such choice.

What reasons could this be?

Social strata: the ways of the heart most times cannot be ascertained, you may have your list and qualities you are looking forward to and your level in the society might limit your scope of association and relationships with people; but when you find love it can break the barriers of class and go beyond what you initially set out to achieve. We have seen the rich marry the rich, we have seen those in the middle class limit the yearnings of their heart to their level and the poor refusing to break free from their cocoon and accept a better lot. Yet again if you let social strata be the reason for your choice, then get ready to dance to the tune they will play for you in that marriage.

Father and Mother's will: when the drama of finding a wife or settling down gets to a point where a father tells you to consider his connection and level in the society before finding that one that pleases your heart, then you know our society is warped. You will now have to think of your father's will before popping the small and big questions. A whole new dimension is when a father goes to the point of threatening death if the son/daughter ever tries to disobey his will. He knows you have obeyed all your life, so even for a decision that is 95 % yours still tries to cajole you and make his will come through by issuing threats and blackmails; I will take poison and die, you will lose your inheritance, I will disown you and any other that can dissuade you from your choice and decision.

Kinsmen's judgment: in our African society, marriages hardly happen without the coming together of the many chains of extended families; in fact, that is what makes the traditional weddings needful. So your immediate family will remind you of what people will say when you choose someone that they don't approve of. You can imagine when a hamlet or community decides your happiness or sorrow in marriage. You can play to their tune or not and be happy or be in perpetual misery because your partner does not arouse your intellect and loins till your good old age. You will have aunties who suddenly will care for you and in fact take responsibility for guiding your emotions and the dance your heart is meant to do.

Some decisions can go a long way in deciding the heights you attain in life and one of such is the choice of a marriage partner. There are a thousand and one considerations to make but one of such shouldn't be the situations listed above. Yes, you need your parents consent after due considerations but when they now want to mortgage your life-long happiness for the sake of the family, kinsmen, social strata or tribe; I think that's way beyond the biblical prescription. This issue of tribe happens to be at the crux of our problems in Nigeria yet we allow a passing generation to decide our lot in this 21st century.

Thank God for elders but experience can become obsolete. Don't let the experience of the 50's generation rob you of the happiness and realities of this decade and century. Settle for that man/lady that can put you out of your dilemma at least.

It is **he who finds** a wife that enjoys favour from the Lord.

35.   THE HARDEST JOB IN THE WORLD

Sometimes ago I was going through some political videos o YouTube just to keep abreast with history and how it is being played out in my country Nigeria. I came across one that seemed boring, long and way too political. It was the ministerial screening of our own Mr Femi Fani-Kayode where he was emphatically telling the then-Senate President Ken Nnamani that in his capacity as special adviser to President Obasanjo he had a job to do, and was bound by the office to do his job.

That statement got me thinking and pointed me to an interesting issue and opened my eyes to the situation Mr Fani-Kayode might have found himself in. This is me trying to figure out what was actually in another man's mind by virtue of a statement he made. I will draw out two quick illustrations or better put explain two things.

Firstly, a job and what a job is. You are employed, asked, delegated to carry out an assignment for which you are being paid for. Your employer can afford to tell you to do anything since he is the one paying for such service. He has the cookie. For the job of the special adviser or assistant it is even more difficult and for other jobs where you have to represent your boss; in speeches, expressions, arguments, defence, lies, truths and making those his leading feel good. In essence, you are trying to get into your boss' mind and say what he would say or asked you to say.

Quickly and secondly, we all have a conscience that works daily for those who still have a good and godly one. Otherwise, you can do any kind of job. Our conscience works based on our knowledge of what is good or evil, worthy or worthless, noble or vain; in any case, it checks what you think, say or do.

Putting it all together, if you are in a position of defending another, in actions, misdeeds and deeds, with a conscience that speaks the truth, you will surely find yourself wrestling with your conscience. You have to tell the public a lie to make your boss look good so you could keep your job.

It is, therefore, a threefold battle; the reputation of your boss, your conscience and retaining the job that puts food on your table. Sincerely I pray not to be in such a situation but if I have to be my prayer is for the wisdom of God to be practically present to lead me. Also, those you are talking to (the public) won't see it in the light that you have to do your job or under instructions to say what you said. You then find yourself taking another person's bullet.

Finally, this piece was done to paint the picture of its title and not in any way insinuating that the characters mentioned found themselves in such situations.

36.   WHAT IF DAVID CAMERON'S FANTASTICALLY CORRUPT STATEMENT IS JUSTIFIABLE?

It is true that British Prime Minister, David Cameron made a statement citing Nigeria and Afghanistan and Nigeria as being fantastically corrupt. This was at the Anti-corruption summit held in London which also had in attendance the Nigerian President, Muhammadu Buhari; who is known for his anti-corruption stance. Your grievance as a Nigerian has been based on the situation and circumstance that such a statement came forth and maybe from whom it came from also because most Nigerians agree that corruption is ravaging our nation. Our president, in fact, won the heart of many in the last elections due to his long-standing views about it.

Now to the statement that had everyone talking and many bickering; Nigeria and Afghanistan are "fantastically corrupt". There might be more explanations from the Prime Minister but that was the hashtag that hit the trend maps. I took out time to find out other words that have been used to describe fantastically (ally) and these are what I found; extremely good, bizarre or strange or unique, incredible, extremely, etc.

To be corrupt popularly has to do with diverting public funds and resources for personal gain. This is true but for some time I have been saying we need to redefine corruption and possibly broaden the scope of its existence and operations. People are quick to tag the high-profile men and women in politics as those who are perpetuating the worst form of corruption in the land while neglecting the little things that go on in the private sector that sometimes surpasses what happens in government. No one was born corrupt, we are taught that our minds are in tabula rasa form, with nothing learnt or imbibed; but over time we start learning' both good and evil.

Before anyone will have the audacity to take huge sums of money meant for the good of other people, he/she must have been exhibiting such as a young man/ woman. Don't we have associations in schools and universities where students do away with the association's money without biting an eyelid? Is not in this nation that the advent of the internet with all of its benefits became a tool of extorting people from both home and abroad?

In this same country, you hear people call in on radio shows and lament about the stealing that is going down in government or wherever. Also, the emergence of someone from obscurity into riches and eventual politics will have people accusing him of benefitting from inflated government projects and contracts. In the past and in recent times, we find politicians, business owners and bank executives being arraigned in court for various levels of money laundering and mismanagement. Our financial watchdog, the Economic and Financial Crimes Commission make revelations on the extent of robbery of the national cake by a few bulldogs.

We have a President who won an election despite all allegations of qualification, propaganda based on three cardinal areas; economy, security and corruption. A sitting Senate President is being arraigned in court almost every week because of this same issue of corruption. In this same country, we have people who will rather make counterfeit products to sell to people damning the consequence of such actions. Or isn't that corruption also?

 The truth of the matter is that there is a corruption tag on Nigeria and it has been so for many years and we all accept that fact and for our President to be carrying it on his head, then the demon of corruption lives among us. I really don't know the reason for the outbursts; is Nigeria no longer corrupt or does fantastically have one unfounded meaning?

Finally, the President said he doesn't want David Cameron's apology but for Britain to return stolen funds that are in Britain. That alone has gone a long way to buttress the known fact that funds are being stolen in Nigeria and that we are corrupt. This is a truth that doesn't need to be bitter but rather to is accepted and some work was done to reverse the trend. David Cameron may be wrong to have taken a swipe at us like that but it doesn't refute the meaning of his statement.

37. BREXIT VOTE, SELF-DETERMINATION AND THE NIGERIAN SITUATION

The news making the rounds for this weekend is the exit of the United Kingdom from the European Union and there have been reactions from various quarters on what will be the resultant effect. There has been one of migration, economic effects on various economies and a day after the vote the pounds sterling experienced a plunge. The Prime Minister, David Cameron has pushed for the UK to remain in the EU has made his plans to resign later in the year. This also is a lesson for leaders in Africa to know when to let go especially when their principles and moral standing have been bridged and an honour has to be preserved.

Looking at it from a different perspective. While writing this piece, I saw a tweet by a respected Nigerian saying Brexit is what happens when people who are elected to lead fail and allow the people to lead through a referendum. I reacted by saying it is better than allowing them to carry arms and hold the people and government to ransom. As much as we believe in the leader showing the way, a referendum might be a limitation to the concept of democracy; a government of the people, for the people and by the people. So a referendum is more like allowing the people decide which way to go but when a popular vote is totally against the good of all, which becomes a problem.

In Nigeria, we have had contentions that bother on unity, diversity, tribe, religion, ethnicity and that popular slogan, One Nigeria. As much as I don't want to sound pessimistic, I like to think that such contentions will continue for a long time unless we get lucky and the tide changes for our greater good. There is a tension reality in the land even though some of us like to be hopeful and make others see reasons to believe in the Nigerian project even when the majority might have a different opinion.

Sad as it may sound, the concept of a referendum is alien to us in this part of the world so what we know how to do is to carry arms, pick a name, make demands that can't be met, assume that we are speaking for every other person affiliated with the group and eventually cause social unrest. That is the society we have come to accept and we seem to be approaching it the same we have always done; national conferences, the battle between security forces and militants, news of dialogue without dialogue, analysis on television and more of going around the circle with no deterrent for future occurrences.

I remember a President Goodluck Jonathan said in a media chat that no President presides over the disintegration of a country but after much thought, I have come to disagree with him. The United Kingdom might not have experienced a national split but a regional/continental one, which shows that the influence and arguments of a Prime Minister were not enough to sweep the tide to favour his intent. A small difference in votes caused the exit of UK from the European Union.

Could the uncertainty of where the votes swing be the reason while African governments or any Nigerian leader has never put up for a referendum seeing that self-determination protests happen all the time? This is not to say that I am giving up on Nigeria or the principles that set us up as a nation; of unity in diversity, faith in each other, peace for national development and collective progress but because the contentions are getting wilder and more devious.

The measures we are using today to check the rising of groups with dissent opinions about Nigeria have not changed yet we keep applying them year after year. If we are not collected in our actions, programs, plans and aspirations our progress will be slow and more like a double step forward and three backwards. The times for half measures are long over and we can't keep doing the same things and expect the same result; a wise man calls that insanity. We need a different approach that can work in the long-term and benefits all parties and stakeholders.

38.   A FACTIONAL PDP AND A CREATED OPPORTUNITY

I have been so engrossed in my work as an architect, reading and writing more that I refuted an assertion by a colleague that the main opposition party in Nigeria, Peoples Democratic Party are divided and pitched into two major factions. Interestingly, these factions just held two different conventions at different locations in the country; Ali Modu Sherrif group in Port Harcourt and Jerry Gana/Ibrahim Mantu group in Abuja.

The situation seems more like a déjà vu of the events of 2013 when the party first hit the rocks and that mighty house yet again proved that a divided one (house) can't stand for long. The series of events at that time started the chain reaction that would sack the party as the ruling party that boasted of 60 years rulership despite the height of irresponsible leadership. You can imagine how they regarded Nigerians, to expect us to keep voting them in for yet another 40 years more.

As the people would have it and as some other political parties maximized the opportunity of a merger to form a bigger party, a new ruling party emerged in the last 2015 general elections with majorities in both chambers of the national assembly and across the states. These events have proved that politics and elections can be a matter of maximizing opportunities of time and history.

 In what has been a major tussle for the leadership of the party since 2014 from Bamanga Tukur to present chairman of the party; Ali Modu Sherrif another opportunity might have been created and those who choose to take it might smile come 2019 general elections and beyond. You might be asking what this opportunity is. It is an opportunity for the emergence of another party or possible merger of smaller parties or a formation of a youth party that will play a viable role as the major opposition for today's democratic dispensation.

No nation is governed effectively and efficiently based on a one-party system where the opposition is virtually dead and inactive to the demands expected of them. As much as the opposition can be a likely threat to the ruling party, a responsive government will always welcome suggestions, views and ideas from other quarters if they are to govern well enough. A government might sometimes get involved in ruling without actually knowing the pulse of the people they are ruling; it then falls to the opposition to make them realize where they are going wrong.

The PDP is a respected party when it comes to the calibre of people that make up their fold but if their personal ambition for power, relevance and authority cannot hold them together to the point of concessions and compromise for colleagues; then they can't provide parallel solutions for the government in power. The country needs a platform and party that can call the APC-led government to order and the present state of the PDP cannot fulfil that onerous task.

Like I said, politics as a game of numbers can also be a game of maximizing opportunities and I am confident that the present factionalism in the PDP has created an opportunity for another platform to emerge. 2019 is not far from us and if such platform is able to play the real role of opposition politics by providing concrete solutions when the ruling party seems to have faulted, they will have gained momentum and followership before the next generation elections.

39.   REDEFINING AND MAXIMIZING YOUR NETWORK

Sometimes I was in need of a raw material to start off a business and from all indication, the material was not in view but I needed to make sure I cleared my doubts about its unavailability. I could travel around the country looking for this material, it won't be wise to do that for something you are just trying to start off and build. So I began thinking of who I could reach out across the country to check their locations for me and interestingly I remembered those to actually call for it. I told them what I needed, got feedback on whether it was available or not and that was I had maximized my network of friends and family to achieve something that was important to me.

There is popular saying that your network determines your net worth; this is certainly true but it all depends on who you regard as being part of the network. These days there are many events that guarantee you opportunities to network especially as young adults but that should not be the limit of those you should network with. In those calls, I made majority were people I knew way back as a child in my elementary and secondary (high) school days. These were people I had a relationship people, people I call on periodically to ask about their welfare and also celebrate with them when they do.

It is important for one to have the following in mind;

- Your childhood friends can be great assets later in your adult and work life. They will prove to be invaluable later in life when you have to pursue new endeavours for your life and career. They will support you in family matters, business affairs, political/leadership quests, they can be your first clients and customers in that business you will intend to start.

- You also need to understand that every phase one passes through in life brings new people into your life for a reason which you might not know then. As much as possible, try and prove yourself worthy of character where they are, build trust, build confidence, establish your integrity and most of all build and value your relationships with them.

- You also need to avoid regarding them as your spare tyres; by that, I mean calling on them only when you need something or are in trouble. Nothing stops you from picking up your phone and placing a call over to them and if that's too much, social media sites are there. If you see them online on Facebook chat them up, catch up on old times, drop a word on their birthdays and celebrate them when they reach a milestone in life.

People wonder how I still keep in touch with people I knew as far back as when I was a child but they never know it is for reason. Burning bridges is not only when you offend people alone, keeping a distance can also mean you don't value them. So your network is not limited to people you meet in high profile events alone but everyone you ever met.

40.   WHAT READING SHOULD MEAN TO YOU

Reading is one major skill or endeavour that we all one way or the other have to learn to do and also continue to do in our daily lives. It starts with the learning of the English alphabet or that of any other language, the formation of words, spellings, and the reading of full sentences. In fact to pass through an education system in the world today, one must learn to read and definitely write. Interestingly, reading has gone beyond schooling or passing an exam; people now read after school in order to inspire, motivate, and gain knowledge and also to learn new skills. The knowledge economy and self-publishing have made it possible for books to be published at ease and for people to learn new things about other people, culture, profession and geography.

Reading for me is not just about the words and their meaning alone, there is more to it and I will share some of it in this piece. Let me state that there are many books one can find out there and of various genres and topics; you can have spiritual, motivational, inspirational, political, history, fictional and a lot more. Depending on which you pick up to read, I am sure experiences are different.

What then should reading mean to you?

The Author's Mind

When you read a book by a particular author, it is an opportunity to get into the subconscious and thinking faculty of that author. It somewhat can be a privilege knowing the ruminations in another person's mind. In connecting to his mind you are not only reading the words of the text alone because if you read very well you will also see/hear things that the author didn't say in the book or what direction his argument is going.

So when you read one must open his/her mind to be able to connect to what the author is trying to say and what he intended to say but willfully omitted to probably provoke your thought your mind. People who write cannot possibly write all they intend to put down in one book but when you read with a second ear, you can connect to those things they didn't actually put down.

Asides reading the words of the author one must analyze, rethink, and see whatever is written in another perspective and dimension. As much as we want to learn from the writer, we must think on what we read in order to see what other inspiration you might learn from your own analyses.

Reading to acquire knowledge should never be a straight-jacketed affair rather we must look at it from a 4-dimensional angle, that way you can have access to certain things the writer didn't mention.   Putting it differently one can actually have an idea of what was in the real manuscript that isn't included in the final print.

41.   WHY IS DEMOCRACY THIS OPINIONATED?

Who in God's name do you want to listen to as a political leader? It is not like business leadership where you know that the company is yours or you are the one who will bear the major brunt of the failure of that business. This is unlike political leadership where you are seen as the manager of the resources entrusted into your hands for four to eight years and everyone seems to have their idea on moving the nation forward in the name of democracy. a government of the people, by the people and for the people; Abraham Lincoln did justice to this.

Could it be that in his time opinions were not that much, or yes we didn't have social media or the internet space that is liberal like breathing in oxygen? Abraham Lincoln was known to gauge public opinion through various means; subordinates, newspapers, visits to the White House and so on but one would think the complexity that was not as it is today.

Today it is high on a different level and with the internet and more recently the proliferation of blogs and websites getting more liberal and inexpensive, political leaders I will say are getting confused on what to actually do (with numerous views). The parameters for leadership or meeting economic needs are numerous; there is no cutout rule of thumb or how we should fix our problems or better still limited options to choose from in meeting economic or political needs. In fact, the options we have are as many as the population of the country because everyone is saying something or has his/her prescription for fixing the economy.

It won't be out of place to posit that nation-building, economic policies, social programs, political structures are based on trial and error because why are we sure that the present economic idea or philosophy is best we would ever have? Why is the opinion of political leader A any better than those of political leader B? That, of course, is a limitation of democracy that every tom, dick and harry can influence what happens in the nation.

In addition to this, is the issue of many aides that help in shaping the actions of a President or Governor and he/she has to take a decision based on the divergent views. The only solution to this will be to have a leader who is capable of all ramifications. A leader who presides over the affairs of millions of people needs to be good at what he does and most importantly have an idea on how the various sectors work rather depending on ministers and aides to dictate the tone.

42.   YOUTH EMPLOYMENT: WHAT MY GENERATION HAS BECOME

Within a space three months, I received four invitations by different people to different independent business summits where you will be taught on starting your own business. I expected something that will focus on proven business principles that one can judiciously apply expecting to have results later. In fact, just on a particular week, I got an invitation of such on Whatsapp asking me to be part of a business venture and investment. I obliged but still found out it is the same old thing I have been invited to.

What then is this business idea that keeps coming back like is my calling to do it? I am quite sure someone has already guessed what it is.

Network Marketing! Yes, you were quite right.

There won't be any need to go into the details of that since it is a popular concept in business strategy or in selling a product. Have you also noticed that such products are neither high-end consumer goods or neither will those at the Bottom of the Pyramid (BOP) be able to afford them? That is one major disadvantage of such products and why people like me are sceptical about joining.

Let me dwell a bit on the bottom of the pyramid. These are people who are considered poor or whom the UN says live on less than $2 a day. They have a limitation in going for luxury goods and items and there is a huge population of such people in Africa and other developing nations like India, South America, Asia, etc. So their population is already a market (a huge one at that) for those who will understand their needs, capability, purchasing power and develop products that can fit into their taste and level. This is a whole new discovery I made some time ago even though I had wanted to start something small that is scalable over time and with constant product sales. A business that is able to offer a product that covers the various classes of people (low class, middle class and high class) has an unlimited potential to keep growing and expanding.

You can decide to call that a limitation of networking marketing businesses that are migrating to Africa. If you must succeed exceedingly here you must target the largest population of low or middle-income earners by selling products that are within their purchasing power.

Going further on this, when I see the products that are sold by these companies I also observe they are mostly for wellness, healthy living, cosmetics, and are basically made from herbs. The raw materials used in making them can be found here in much abundance and I have been wondering why those products can't be made here to target the huge population of poor people (whom I'm sure desire to live healthily). Someone will be sceptical about our business environment but the truth is there is no place where the business environment is perfect and working optimally. It only takes those who are determined to find opportunities in those limitations of doing business in your immediate environment.

The way our businesses are in Nigeria and Africa is such that people are more concerned about giving out an amount of money and getting something extra in return. Not many people want to sit down, plan, and develop a system that can run efficiently and effectively as a business model or entity. The ones who have achieved it are doing great but the other group who want the cash at hand are more in number.

As much as I desire to be wealthy materially and have some good cash, I also long to build something with my mind, develop a system, a business model that people can learn from even after I'm gone.

43.   REFOCUSING OUR EDUCATION

Education is the most powerful weapon which you can use to change the world.

-Nelson Mandela

The many aspirations and activities of man are mostly targeted towards making the world a better place either for oneself or for others, but what is important is that we are changing to something better even as challenges arise. One of the many ways to change someone is to change their thinking, give them a new experience, expose them to something new and worthwhile, and make them have a feel of something better. Give them a reason to see the world differently; then you would be one your way to changing the world through these individuals.

It is no news that Nigeria as it is, is in the era of change where an opposition party moved to ruling party on that mantra of change. Yes, a lot needs to change in Nigeria especially in the area of security and our collective cohesion to rebuild our nation. Of top discussions in the news are on the onslaughts of Fulani herdsmen and their tirade of inhumane acts on fellow Nigerians. It further escalated to the recent killings in Enugu communities in South-East Nigeria and many are beginning to see it as a war between a section of the country and another. This proves that we are yet to learn our lessons from history.

Any attempt of reprisal will plunge the nation in a whole new level of chaos and anarchy simply because we are quick to announce our affiliations in tribe and ethnicity neglecting the greater good of calling ourselves, Nigerians. As much as these people pose a serious threat to national security and the President is expected to declare a war on them, we need to deal with the root cause of the problem; that way we can have a lasting solution.

A man who feels that taking another's life means nothing or that such an act is justifiable obviously has had the wrong orientation, exposure and upbringing. No one is born a murderer and terrorist but the society and what we imbibed into others goes a long way in creating such individuals. People who get involved in crime are partially justified because they are unemployed or idle, blame others like government for their woes, are frustrated to point despair, etc. The case of the Fulani herdsmen is not totally because of joblessness or idleness but it is a situation of orientation and exposure since rearing their cattle keeps them busy. You and I know how much one of their cattle can go for, so beyond poverty, lack or want, their profession has no value for others and whatever they possess.

The government is working to develop grazing areas across the country which is laudable but it will have a greater effect if these men are given a different kind of orientation about life, values, business and being another Nigerian's keeper. Despite being violent they still can be spoken to and convinced against what they have been known to practice for years which they can equally pass on to the younger ones that follow them around.

According to Aristotle, the purpose of education is to teach one how to earn a living and how to live too. Any endeavour that one involves despite the worth yet is lacking in right values has no standing in the society. If you think you can run a business using double standards then your time is limited in the market.

The challenges we face today were not with us some years ago but now they are with us. We are seeing all these challenges today because of changing times. So also we need to change what we teach in our schools, churches, mosques, workplaces and other groups we find ourselves. Our world seems to be changing without us changing the way we approach issues or what we learn.

History is history is what it is because of what it had, the ideas that existed and what we learned too; the present is what it is because of what is learning and the ideas we have now and to get ready for the future there are things to learn so we can adapt to it. As a matter of urgency, we need to be answering the questions of the future now to avoid being overwhelmed by uncertainty and lack of preparedness for it.

If this change is ever going to work, and if we expect it to work effectively, efficiently and sustainably, then there is a need to address our educational shortfalls urgently. Let us imbibe a new culture of learning to meet up with the demands of changing times.

44.   TEACHER DON'T TEACH ME NONSENSE

Let me tell you a series of stories.

One day while in the University, I came across a friend from another department but same college building and she was grieving, sad and broken. She couldn't even respond to my question of what was wrong with her and I understood I had to walk till she is able to talk.

Later that evening, we got talking on Facebook and she opened on why she was in that depressing state with emotions running within. A lecturer had said some bad words to her, of not being good, smart or intelligent for the course he was teaching her.

All I had to was to reassure to look beyond what lecturers say; that their judgment about life and success ends in their class, and nothing more.

She was not the first person that was going through such and many people get run down by lecturers who are either supervisor of projects or part of a defence jury. Rather than correct to build up, encourage, guide, and inspire bashing feels more appropriate for them.

With all credence to the Fela, I will say to you lecturers, "Teacher Don't Teach Me Nonsense".

Education has many benefits, the world, in fact, needs more people who are in the professional fields than ever. We need scientists, research, we need to explore the potential of the earth, what nature and God have endowed us with and the proven way to this is to research, seeking questions, and development. We need students and graduates who have their self-esteem still intact if they are doing programs like Microbiology or another course that are disregarded.

Unfortunately, our universities and school systems have degenerated to institutions where tutors and lecturers frustrate students while venting their personal frustrations that might be domestic in nature. The Western world has taught us that the people like Bill Gates, Albert Einstein succeeded beyond what other people think of them but here we have lecturers who lord it over on students because he/she has the power to keep you as a student for untold years.

No thanks to a system that works on its own.

Any teacher that feels good disparaging a student needs not to be one. He/she can go and deal with his wards same way. A teacher should inspire you to think with the right questions posed to you, not necessarily to give the perfect answer but to enjoy the process of thinking things through till an answer comes. The process of everything is where the gold lies and forget every lie that tells you that the end justifies the means.

To the Students

Don't allow yourself to be seen as unserious because if you are laid you will need more than encouraging in love but reproof as well. If on the other hand, you know you are committed to your studies then learn not to allow any teacher no matter his attainment run down your esteem. Your esteem needs to be in check for you to think, endure and find opportunities in any rough journey that life will offer you.

On a professional level as an employee now, you will find bosses that are worse than thorns in the flesh. They practically go beneath your skin into the born marrow and if you are not careful to the heart of emotions. A boss or an employer most times are affected by the stagnation of the company or the thought that he needs to pay salaries every month. That is understandable but not justifiable to say words like "you are useless" to an employee.

Employers' rights do not exceed that point of determining what and who someone is. It is apparently beyond his scope of work as a supervisor, manager, founder or CEO. If the person is not doing the job satisfactorily, deal with the job rather than taking it personally but if it must be personal then it should show care and concern. After all, you are paying him to work for you and the money should be meeting a need and family is part of that need.

To conclude, everyone especially if you are under someone needs to be careful of those you are allowed speak some words in your direction or to your hearing. They have a way of getting into your subconscious that you start thinking that you are actually useless. Psychologists can explain biologically but Proverbs 23:7 tells us that "as a man thinketh in his heart, so his he."

So if you allow someone place a negative or inferior thought into your mind, you might be on your way to processing it to reality.

Guard your heart, for out of it are the issues of life (Pro. 4:23)

45. CONCRETE APPLICATIONS OF NIGERIA'S STRENGTH IN DIVERSITY

The diversity of Nigeria is one area that has been a blessing with the same measure of challenges for us as well. With over 250 ethnic groups and 400 languages, two major religions and the peculiarities of individual character, you can as well say that Nigerians as a country are individually diverse. In all these understanding of how different we all are, there has never been a definite application of it to our benefit practically except when we need to discuss ownership of this entity called Nigeria.

Diversity can only be a strength when it makes us stronger but when it only takes us down the path of corruption, nepotism, greed, violence and hate then it makes us weak as well. In taking a look at religion as a factor, we have two major ones; Islam and Christianity and we both worship in different days of the week; Fridays and Sundays respectively. Periodically within the week, the two religions of various churches and mosques gather to honour God and share our problems with Him.

This distinction in the worship of God can be used in a manner whereby Muslims can take the place of Christians at work and vice versa when any of them are away to pray or some things that are unavoidable. The times when one person or two are absent from the office due to religious reasons can be filled in by another party who share same values of moving the organization and nation forward. For instance, in petrol filling stations I have seen some that sell on Sundays while others don't but we can maximize the fact that our Muslims brothers don't worship on that day and involve them in such work while the Christians go to worship.

Fridays, which is the day of Jum'at prayers can be structured in such way that Christians do not relax because Muslims have to go pray by 2 pm. While the seek God in prayer others who don't participate can be involved to keep the system running without reduced productivity or efficiency. The whole idea of this is that for the fact that we take religion very seriously and honour God with our presence and more, it should not rob us of work time and be an alibi for not achieving daily and weekly milestones.

Days back while driving down I saw some people trying to fix a streetlight that needed some repairs and with crane high up, traffic movement of cars was affected. In other similar instances, I have seen waste management workers doing their work and this clearly disrupts traffic or cause air pollution with so many incinerators moving from one end of town to another. Why can't such people that do these jobs be empowered to do such jobs at night and no one will disrupt them and they won't affect others as well.

Like I said earlier, we are individually diverse and some people can work well at night while some during the day. There are moments of energy, strength and vigour and it will unwise to think that everyone has it at the same times. We have been on this journey as a country dealing with diversity as a strength largely in speeches and show of traditional attires yet our challenges of ethnic bigotry keep holding us back.

There are many other applications to this; another is in the sharing of ideas in offices and organizations. Rather than have people from various ethnic locations and backgrounds to share views on the reality of life where they are coming from we choose to play nepotism. A bank that needs to open a new branch needs to understand the territory or new location and an indigene or one familiar with the area will do well in telling the prospects in such areas.

The bane of national journey and progress is largely due to the fact that we focused on unity when unity is not our problem when it is not a virtue that is universal and is prone to compromise. Diversity is a strength when we allow it respect virtues of social justice, equity, honour and sacrifice. We can be tap into this strength of differences of backgrounds, exposures, mindsets (good) and move forward faster and as one country.

We are either focusing on the weakness of diversity or tapping into the strengths that lie within each and every one of us.

46.   WHY THE PURPOSE OF UNITY IS OUR FIRST CHALLENGE IN NIGERIA

The word "Unity" even before independence has been a sacred word in the terms of Nigeria's socio-political history. It is the root of our nationhood as shown in our national motto it appears to be the purpose of our creation and independence. Hearing of unity many will think it is for a greater good, many think that our diversities can be harnessed properly if unity is resounded like any other word whether in the economic or political scene. In recent times, it has been rephrased to, "Nigeria's Unity being non-negotiable".

Without trying to live in self-denial I use to cherish the concept of unity and how it should be the basis for our growth and how it will be the rallying point for social cohesion, faith in each other and ourselves, and the major factor for peace and progressive development (Unity and Faith, Peace and Progress). And today after four years of learning and observing the trend and asking questions about Nigeria, I have concluded that unity as a word is our first and major challenge and all others stem from the resounding call and mention of Unity, National Unity and what have you.

Unity of Purpose as citizens is not a bad idea and this is only possible when we recognize the fact that we might have cultural and racial differences but we are same as Nigerians, humans and a nation under heaven and God. Unfortunately, what unity does and has been doing since amalgamation is to show our differences more than addressing the challenges that come with it. Unity makes it clear and obvious that we are not just one Nation of

Nigerian citizens but we are a country of over 250 ethnic nationalities and 400 languages. Yes, unity is there to make us look beyond those difference but it does more to say that we different and divided.

It is in the efforts to unite as Hausa, Igbo or Yoruba or Ijaw, Efik, Nupe, Ibibio, Edo, Benin et al more vicious challenges like nepotism and favouritism start coming in. It is a unity that breeds corruption when one is obligated and conscious that he is different from another person who is not his tribe and must compromise for his kit and kin. When there are a notion and fixed mindset on how different we are, one has a likelihood to break laws and rules for those who are same as he/she is.

It is this same unity that teaches people to be religion-conscious, to see a distinction that being Nigerian cannot solve. We start making decisions terrible decisions for God in the name of religious differences, bias and unity that sounds loudly in Christianity and Islam. Unity might seem sacred but unfortunately, it has caused more damage than good and I will tell you why.

Why didn't we choose other terms and mottos like social justice, honour, strength and equity? These all are universal, immune to corruption so long as we understand what they really mean by an explicit definition. Whereas unity underlines our differences, others like social justice and equity will treat issues as good and bad, will treat issues as humane and inhumane. We won't have to deal with tribe and religion so long as one goes contrary to the law that negates social justice, equity and honour he/ she will face the law. Universally accepted terms will do a lot to erode the differences between tribe, religion and forces of nepotism and favouritism.

As much as Nigeria needs structural adjustments in our federalism which bothers more on political and economic issues, we fundamentally need to address the social issues. We need to define the things we hold dear as a country. It is the broken social system that makes our leaders show condolences to foreign nations when terror happens while many die every day on our shores. I have asked myself several times about what really is the value we place on a life in this country especially if the person is not related to you.

What is Nigeria's rating of the life of her citizens?

Any efforts to restructure without dealing with the fundamental issues of principles, values and collective and individual goals and aspirations will only be as futile as the word futility. Let unity be expunged from our national life, let us shift focus from trying to unite, have faith and ensure peace before progress. That is a long road to achieving greatness. We can achieve it speedily by accepting to do good and working against bad in all ramifications.

47.   MINDS IN BOXES

The mind is regarded as so many things; it gives you what you put inside it, it is limitless, it is like a spring of water that never runs dry, it is unpredictable, can move in any direction, is capable of attaining the level of divinity, the mind can be seen as an amoeba that can take up no shape. However, the infinite extent of the mind is only dependent on each person's choice and how one decides to allow their flow.

We are told not to box it up, we are told to think outside the box, many have said we should think around the box and taking it further we are also told to think like there is no box. Whichever way a mind goes or the height each attains depends on how they are willing to stretch it. The elasticity of the mind does not have a plastic stage because it has the capacity to keep stretching, expanding, gaining strength and growth.

In this piece, though sounding philosophical and inspirational I will like to get subjective about how we need to remove every box when it comes to trying to understand what happens around us in the society. The mind needs to move away from any boxes to understand what happens in the corridors of power, business, and politics and in our government houses. Not everything is black and white and the people who find themselves at the theatre of the power show have minds that are equally elastic and infinite.

We need to see our politicians and leaders as people who do practically everything that citizens do; they eat, sleep, talk, dance, make calls, live in houses and homes, watch TV, can get angry, use the toilet, feel lazy and sick and whatever you can think of that humans are able to do in their closets or in the public. The world today and the politics that is defining the tide of events is being made, unfortunately, annoyingly and frustratingly interesting with the fake news, propaganda and social media.

It is more unfortunate that the ones that news is targeted at have become gullible to the point that one can believe when they are told something that pertains to themselves. Fake news and propaganda thrive because of so many things and one of it is the inability for mankind to use their minds. The inability to unleash our minds from the boxes that envelopes it.

If a government in Africa decides to release statements to the public because they are expected to, what makes you think they do exactly what is issued in those press releases? For the mere fact that politics is seen as a game for the satisfaction of vested interests that are unholy and unjust should tell you that what is said or seen is not always what is done or right.

It is the restriction of our minds in a box that makes some of us think that a President or Governor cannot place a personal call to a Senate President or Party leader or an opposition candidate to reach some compromises or tell them to do something different from what was discussed in an earlier meeting. Yes, the President or Governor can make calls in their bathrooms, their study, private rooms and quarters without anyone knowing about it. It is only in recent times that people started seeing how the seat of government looks like in Nigeria. The full appearance of the President's office is not known by the public or even the media. The security checks in Aso Rock requires you to drop of any cellphones at some points meaning that taking pictures is completely out of it. The images your eyes capture are enough for as long as your memory can carry you.

We need to release our minds from the bondage of unseen boxes that limits our critical analyses of events, media reports, Presidential directives, political games and activities so that we don't fall into believing everything including the obvious craps. The thing with failing to think these things through before believing them is that after so many dramas and activities from the same person, office or party you will discover incoherence and any efforts to defend them will only make you look really stupid.

Thanks to our journalists and media personnel but they are in business to make money and if the quick means to that is simply deceiving a gullible and unenlightened public then is no big deal for them. The end in sight for them goes beyond justifying the means.

The corridors of power and what happens there is like the beating of one's heart; it is constant, something is always happening and the media never loses out daily on news headlines. There is always a news report; a President saying this, a launch, a commissioning, a diplomatic visit and many more. On the other flipside of things, there are things that the media is kept out of; the behind the scene moments, the agreements, the oaths taken over handshakes, white papers, in 5 minutes, sitting or standing, in person or over the phone or internet.

Public officials can decide to chat with each other regarding a highly important issue that can affect even the poorest on the street in worse condition that he/she (the poor) was. Politicians don't lie because of what they say or not say or do; the lie can come in telling you something else on television but actually having something different discussed in their homes. In this time and era when some people can skillfully say things that are different from what their heart pulse/beat is with the right kind of temperament and emotional control, then expect nothing less from what happens in private rooms and toilets.

We have moved into a generation that is quick to believe things that are apparent lies from those who understand the gauge of shaping public opinion and perception. Our minds need a flow path that boxes cannot limit. You don't have to know what someone did or said to know what he is capable of doing or might have done without you seeing or knowing. We need to save an ugly trend of fake aggregators and a public that believes hook, line and sinker.

Start thinking things through, start asking questions, starting being empathic, start painting scenes and possible scenarios of what a human being like yourself can do. The mind is a goldmine that cannot be left in the box. Non-usage of it causes negative effects like a lack of motivation and a positive effect will make life far easier.

48. WHILE U.S FACES FAKE NEWS, THIS IS WHAT WE FACE IN NIGERIA

If you throw a question to the public on if social media has done a lot of good or harm you are likely to get many answers that will say good or bad, both including those who used it wrongly to create good for themselves will have something to say. Whichever the case, there are pros and cons but for the sake of this piece, I will be sharing with you the different shades that the use of social media has taken. The U.S is battling with fake news under President or as he describes those that come after his administration but for in Nigeria, we are dealing with some scarier things that make fake news look less dangerous.

Fake news is simply wrong reporting of events and things as they occur either for opinion sharing sake, to get a better view of things or being biased and prejudiced against a section of the society or individuals. Interestingly, fake news is also in the Nigerian media space but you can explain it better as media propaganda. Such propaganda is scary and risk because people spend hard currency to promote them, make them trend and create conversations that cause more harm than good.

We are in a generation where young people have been reduced to survival modes; people basically after what to eat, lay hold upon as the day goes by. The generation has been conditioned to so many rat races that we are more concerned about outpacing each other when the real enemies and their cronies have the day, months and years to keep celebrating. Social media; Twitter, Facebook, Instagram, LinkedIn and others have done so much good; however the wrongs maybe in equal proportions or more.

Before I proceed to discuss these challenges that are clearly dangerous, let me state that the cons of social media are different for each platform like Twitter or Facebook each have their areas of challenge.

Pseudo Realities

People use social media to portray pseudo-realities about their conditions, real experiences, and true stories about their lives. It is as if photography (no offence to our wonderful curators of history) has made it possible for people to share falsehood about their lives when they can alter, filter and enhance whatever they want. The danger of this might not be against them but those who will out of ignorance and being gullible believe the social media flashy folks who are practically far from what a filtered picture presents.

Cashtivism

People have moved from activism for good (not because they are jobless or without work) to what is now called Cashtivism on Twitter. People go offline to do whatever they do in private like getting paid and wired transfer and come online to defend evil because of their soul, life and bond are at stake to defend even the indefensible. This is still the survival mode of trying to food on the table, conscience is dead and seared with a red-hot iron. So you see people who should be role models caught in the deep ocean of defending wrong just because they have collected cash to do and must keep their bargain with politicians and the cabals that hold our siege.

Wrong and Dangerous Narratives of History

Nigeria is today on the threshold of history and a time like this requires that citizens understand and appreciate a good part of their history. People need to know where we are coming from, the mistakes of the past, the sacrifices of our founding fathers and the various threats we have had to endure as a nation. Unfortunately, it is not so. We even have something more threatening and that is the dangerous narratives of lies, deceits, and sentimental narration of history. People prefer to tell lies on social media for cheap popularity or because they have to write or post something online. Not understanding the history of our country is a threat but giving wrong narratives about history is a greater threat than the former. Fakes news is fake because people distort facts and figures to suit their special interests which are clearly selfish.

Untruthful Opinions

This is the one that is heart-breaking not because everyone should have the same level of knowledge and understanding but because the ones that share wrong and untruthful opinions do so without remorse, teachable when you correct beyond any doubt and are hardcore fanatics. As much as everyone is entitled to their opinions, not every opinion is entitled to sharing. You don't just cook up things because of a hurting past and make it the rule of life; it can be the rule of your life. However, opinions have been proven to be cheap and the thing that matters today is the conviction that is equally truthful. People can have devilish convictions that give them cheap and timely relevance and they fade away from history.

While social media has been a force for good in many ways, it has equally used to cause damages that might never be repaired. The greatest of all the threats is the threat to future generations; unborn, still growing and young people who have taken to social media for knowledge and enlightenment. The future and those who will drive it are threatened by a preceding generation that is clearly chasing dreams without an understanding of the past and the present.

49. LIKE DIGITAL TECHNOLOGY, POLITICS ALSO NEEDS DISRUPTION

The world, no doubt is already digital, but in this age of the digital, some animals are more equal than others. There is a deliberate attempt by new entrants into the technological ecosystem to disrupt and challenge what you can popularly call tech status quo. This wave of disruption is seen in many emerging nations like China, Singapore, India, Nigeria, Kenya, Rwanda and across continental boundaries.

It is a good development and laudably so.

However, despite the advances being made by resilient businesses, idealists and entrepreneur, the political scene seems not to be making progress in the business sector. Yes, politics should be managers and drivers of what happens in the business scene through policies that engender growth but despite their leading role there seems to be more bad news emanating from the conduct of their affairs.

In Nigeria, for instance, and in many other countries perhaps, what happens around us has a way of shifting the chief blame and fault on the government or those at the helm of government. We seem to be receiving more embarrassing news than those that have to do with international fraud or cybercrime. Errors from government and leaders have more drastic effects on every sector the economy yet (in Africa), we are yet to find a handful of leaders who can champion a disruption of the political scene beyond wealth, money and material benefits.

In Nigeria, the two major political parties have lost the confidence of the people. In fact, you can say that the political class has a trust deficit among the teeming population of Nigerians. People are frustrated to the point of preferring to mind their businesses and breaking natural laws and the ones equally set up by the government. Paying tax seems to be a seed that generates nothing return, so you can call it a burden on the shoulders of many. While the frustrations are still ongoing, while the PDP moves from one-midnight meeting and courthouse to another; and while the APC try to galvanize themselves to fulfil promises made without data and strategy on the ground, many more Nigerians are wondering what the next election year in 2019 would bring.

We are not even talking about the agitations for secession and issues threatening that almighty law and caption that reads, "the indivisibility of the Nigerian state", or that corrupt-style of unity that has been like hovering evil storm above us. We are at the point in history where things seem to be working but in the opposite direction of progress.

We need a bailout politically, socially, economically, spiritually, emotionally and otherwise.

Politically (which should lead these reforms), another party has emerged in the Nigerian scene; Advanced Peoples Democratic Alliance. The name sounds like rechristening of the Peoples Democratic Party while bearing a near similar acronym like the All Progressive Congress.

Having listened to the speech of one of their leaders, Mr Dan Nwanyanwu; a man whom if it is based on what he says has won my respect, I can that he tried to disrupt the narrative of past political parties. He spoke about developing and seeking our raw materials, talking about shifting from agriculture as just farming to production along the value-chain and of course he made reference to women and youth being considered by their political party. Now, this is not a routing for this party but truth be told, the political scene needs a lot of disruption.

In as much as people are saying restructure, divide and secede, if all these are attained either way, if there is no change from the narrative of pettiness to something better and morally acceptable, then is better remain as we have always been. We can invest energy and resources in something that can bring change and meaning to our national life only to revert back to status quo charging furiously to Egypt.

I have heard news of political parties emerging, of INEC being thronged with more work of registering new platforms and we can only hope that they can bring a disruption that is not just in speeches and words but through action and policies that helps everyone fulfil their aspirations as Nigerians. We need a disruption that will bring those benefitting from a Nigeria that is not working to their knees. We need a better of force will, courage and determination that can make every cabal of the Nigerian state to defuse completely. We need people that can reset every evil and ungodly mindset about Nigerian government and leadership both home and abroad.

This disruption needs to tend towards utilizing data while making election promises. Data should be the basis of the picture you paint for us in the vision for Nigeria. The big visions that are not strategy-based have proved to be a scam and it is only verifiable and trackable data that can help us fix this emotional robbery that comes with political campaigns and electioneering. We are yet to conduct another census after 11 years yet we keep passing national budgets that are based on ghost citizens that cannot be accounted for, dead or alive. It is either Nigeria as a country works, or we can decide to part ways, after all, the amalgamation document has expired, or the call for agitation keeps getting stronger by the day.

Finally, we are talking about solid minerals and mining and the minister seems not to have done anything tangible that one can see yet (at least I have not). It will a shame on the black intellect and wisdom if, by the time we start exploring our solid minerals, we decide to export it alone without exploring them or simply going the way of oil. This is a major area that needs disruption; maximizing the potentials in our resources, stretching them through research and development initiatives. That is the only way we can be competitive globally, enjoy stress-free FX issues, build a sustainable economy and emerge a world power in a different way.

We are a great nation but potentially so.

50. ANOTHER TALE OF EMPOWERMENT USING GALLONS OF WATER

As if the sorry case of using wheelbarrows and transistor radios as a way of empowering people in states that have huge potentials in many areas, another governor in Nigeria has gone further to belittle the doings of his counterparts in Benue and a Senator from Kaduna by branding 25 litres of water as a tool of empowering young people.

It is also interesting to know that some young people who are enlightened came in defence of these ones that are making a big deal of governance while showing an unfortunate level of incompetence. Wheelbarrows, Transistor radios and gallons of water have been with us for over 2 decades or more. In fact, the radios were used during the war and governor in AD 2017 thinks we the young people should still remain in the times of 1960.

Willie Obiano and his Anambra have been in the news lately, even the former governor Peter Obi has refused to go into political oblivion despite leaving office 3 years ago. Obiano, is in fact, seeking for a second tenure in office and such news is emanating from his borders and state. Though he can decide to call this a political blackmail by opponents, in as much as his government has not issued a counter-statement, then the public is allowed to rate him accordingly.

The way I see this news that is simply heart-wrenching is this; if I was to be in those states and like those young people and maybe enlightened with a degree from their state universities, a governor will seek to empower me by giving me a wheelbarrow or a gallon of water. While I still try to figure out the reason for the water gallons, I can conclude that a lack of education is also foisting lack of esteem on many young Nigerians who are definitely unaware of what other young folks are creating in other nations. We need not go far, Rwanda is a good example of where a nation that suffered genocide recently is leading Africa in so many ways that you deem as sustainable. Yes, Nigeria was rated as having the highest GDP in Africa but this was in a midst of high inequality, over 60 percent poverty rate and other issues of security and corruption that probably over bloated the GDP.

For these leaders that make a mess of governance and human dignity, they need to have their personalities reexamined starting from childhood, upbringing, business and especially the education they got before seeking to lead us as Nigerians. There is a no defence under heaven and the earth that can be enough to rationalize such and an action of poverty retainment in the name of empowerment. Are we moving forward or we are simply allowing rogues in power to play on our intelligence while the build their families and personal empires. Even though you didn't enter power as a poor man, there is a mandate for governance in politics and which is to uplift people, change lives, give people hope, recreate a failing system, help others to dream and achieve whatever level they can think of and not for you to play on our exposure of where the world is headed.

A generation is shifting and leaving already in Nigeria; the fourth generation of Nigerian leaders is emerging and the doings of the passing ones will remain fresh in our minds.

Why am I saying this?

Some millennials will start occupying leadership positions soon and before you start thinking like your fathers, you need to be reminded that the world has moved on and left us behind and we are eager to catch up. We don't need people whose thinking faculties are simply ankle deep presiding over us when we can get the best of leadership that the humans can offer. Just like we are resisting these old ones today, we would resist their sons and protégés the same way and forcefully so.

How dare you try to mortgage the future of our children while crookedly safeguarding yours?

If you know you cannot raise the bar of governance and leadership very high, please stay clear of politics and remain in your comfort zones let those who are able to take up the saddle.

51. DOES GLOBALIZATION CONSIDER EQUALITY AS WELL?

As much globalization sound formal and academic, I don't intend to make this piece to sound like one. I hope I can drive home my point and argument convincingly without goring anyone's ox.

Definition of a globalization comes with free trade, movement of goods and services, migration and the idea of an interconnected world. This covers countries linking up with others, continents sharing goods and services and the world becoming a global village. It has also been taken to another level with the sharing of data in this knowledge economy and in fact, cybercrime is a way of globalization as one agency website was hacked within the week just at the wake of internet security awareness.

For the purpose of migration, I remember childhood friends and neighbours who have one way or other have found themselves in Europe in search of that old phrase, "where pastures are green". Quite a number of them have college/university degrees yet when they get there; they get involved in works that task physical strength rather than the mind. It is obvious who rules the pack of physical or mind-worker.

I won't also deny the fact that many well-meaning Nigerians are doing great in intellectual work and endeavours but how are actually getting the peak of careers as respected in the US and Europe or wherever they might be.

If globalization is to be seen as something honourable, then it must respect the dignity and ability of all across the world. When a skill is not lacking and education is not in short or the ability to learn is not handicapped, Africans should be given the opportunity to play critical roles in global economies. We can't continue having young men with minds and are teachable working like people in slaves plantations of the 19th century.

Africans might have physical strength but are an intellectual strength is equally stronger when given the opportunity of being trained and equipped.

One of my best movies yet; an Abraham character told us that "till every man is free, then we are all slaves". Till everyone is given the opportunity and freedom of dreaming and achieving, we all are slaves of a global economy. The words of MLK on the content of character holds relevant meaning like the words of Scriptures and this I believe is human and of mankind, irrespective of race and nationality.

If we are building a global economy or village, then each one of us must have equal rights as citizens.

## 52.	WHEN POLITICIANS START MISUSING WORDS

In that revered movie, V for Vendetta, one of the powerful quotes was that Politicians use lies to cover the truth, while writers use them (lies) to the tell the truth.

As much as this is the truth and always self-evident, I think that smarter politicians have taken it to another that seems to be less noticeable by those who choose to focus on the surface of what emanates from their mouth. I have seen the tale of a governor in Nigeria who practically read his inaugural speech from his head; the power of oratory was not in doubt but 6 years down the line his performance has been poor.

And when asked why it is so, he sure always has a perfect defence that seems undebatable. I have seen a former Head of State who uses sentiments of religion and bearing the buck of leadership to avoid telling us what transpired under his watch as President. I have seen lawmakers who are good at giving justifications for delayed passage of bills in a nation where there is urgency for things to get better.

I don't like to call President Trump because he says it the way it is but the new breeds of politicians are quickly adopting the strategy of using oratory, a combination of words to deceive people who can't see beyond the words and where it is coming from.

Have seen a Theresa May's interview and how she confidently avoids answering a question with an explanation that is vaguely vague, indirect and mumbled up. Guess what, that is the new skill and power that is needed to succeed in this after influence and affluence.

All through the civilization of man, words have been known to work magic and perform wonders. The effect is powerful, lasting from one generation to another, holding the same value for those that are timeless. The strength of Gandi and MLK was backed up by the content of their inner man and mind which often reflected through words. With such power, the inspired their generation to action, the world still stand still for them every year.

Hitler might have been a monster consumed with ambition to take over the world but he had followers. His oratorical powers were electrifying, you can't beat that and when you think of him as an enemy, the strength and passion of his speech just change your perception about him.

Why is this skill very important in this time and age?

With it, you can a defence for everything if possible convince one that a black pot is white (Africans will understand this). Words have been adopted by criminals and corrupt men to escape prosecution.

How do you acquire such power?

Very simple.

Study; the good book in 2Tim. 2:15 tells us that by studying you will have what to show. It is a gradual process of building this skill and highly sustainable so long as you can sustain your studying.

53.　　WHILE WE WAIT FOR RESTRUCTURING: OPTIONS BEFORE STATE GOVERNMENTS

The call for the restructuring of Nigeria keeps getting louder as more people join their voices to the conversations surrounding it. This is so because it will be a way of correcting a foundation that has been faulty from the very beginning. It is not working, it is wasteful, highly unsustainable, and socially, economically and politically unjust and it is not adding consistent value or uplifting lives as a government should.

It is also evident that the states and local governments are the ones bearing the major brunt of this dysfunctional system; they owe more salaries, hardly carry out major capital projects, don't have the power to explore their resources, cash-strapped, and more people are deserting them in what we all know as rural-urban migration. There is definitely an urgency of now and until we realize the urgency of how we must do something to help the states start thriving and making slow but steady progress.

In this piece, I will share strategies that states in Nigeria can adopt to rebuild and create wealth for their people that will be sustained over time. Let me also add that states in Nigeria are not the first nation-states that were limited resources (though their limitation is constitutionally enforced), but countries like Singapore and Indonesia had a similar experience but through known strategies and consistency they are now ranked as first world nations all within a timeframe of 50 years.

Strategic Partnerships: This has been proven as a very feasible business/economic strategy both in the private and public sector. Nigerian states can decide to partner with private indigenous businesses and individuals who control a level of wealth that they hardly know how to channel them. A state like Anambra in the South-Eastern part of the country is known to have a huge concentration of wealthy men and women who have taken a simple business like trading to unimaginable heights. It may be simple in nomenclature but they have succeeded in building systems that now span into the corporate business sectors of the economy. Their reluctance in engaging in some programs, I am sure is caused by the style of politicians and their willingness to think of better ways to do more for their people. If a willing government approaches them for a partnership that can achieve three things; give government credit and wealth, create wealth for the businesses and also benefit the common man, I am confident they will gladly be a part of it. Such partnerships can also be extended to expatriates and businesses from other nations and this comes with more sustainable benefits like transfer of skills, knowledge to the local citizens of the state who can continue the work when the expatriates go back to their countries. This also will offer us a transfer of better technology that we might not have known existed in these countries.

Issue-based Education: There is no doubt that the world has moved rapidly in the last decade and half a century. Technology has improved, the knowledge economy has brought with it so many changes in the way we do things especially in other nations and Nigeria must catch up with these developments. It will interest you to know that some schools including basic, secondary and tertiary still run the same curriculum they had since the inception of their schools and you wonder how our students and graduates will be able to compete favourably with others.

It is time state governments start training and shaping their system of education to address present-day challenges that affect their sub-national economies. If there is need to address issues using technology and start-ups, then invest it young people who will drive these by creating solutions. If something like power or infrastructure is a challenge, then more people can be equipped to address this locally without having to involve or expatriates except in special cases of new technology required.

While we wait for the government of the day as led by the federal government and members of the economic and state council to decide on the way forward for us in this country, the states need not relax. They can start thinking of ways to start creating wealth that can help them to be self-sufficient.

Other areas can be an investment in agriculture, the establishment of industries, maximizing the value chain of agriculture to the barest minimum. There are local products like textile, shoes, metal works, etc; that can be explored by states to help drive their economies without over-dependence on allocation from the federal government. Maybe it is the time they start utilizing the allocations to invest in wealth-creating ventures rather than expending them on recurrent expenditures like salaries.

54.   A DIFFERENCE BETWEEN ALIKO DANGOTE AND OTHERS

He is reputed to be the richest African in the world and in fact he has become a household name for many in Nigeria, Africa and the world. His brand and name is one that is almost penetrating the fabric of our national life with the array of products they keep introducing to the market.

From Sugar, flour, pastries, cement, a refinery that is targeted at boosting power in Nigeria; Aliko Dangote is one entrepreneur that is different in a very distinct and unique way and I will share that in this piece.

Now he is not the only billionaire in Nigeria or Africa, much more abound, many have made the Forbes list and much more are joining the ranks but having taken a look at Mr Dangote I can say that there is something he is trying to achieve beyond just building wealth. The many businessmen and women we have are mostly involved in businesses that require importation of products or using raw materials from abroad. They are the ones that get emotional about dollar spike and restrictions and those who have one way or other earned the name 'cabal' for themselves.

They are the ones that paint us as consumers to the western world but an Aliko is different.

His major raw materials are sourced from within our borders. The cement factories he has made use of the large deposits of limestone in our middle belt regions. That gives naira value in the event of exporting the end products of his cement to other nations of the world. The sugar industry is maximizing the value-chain of sugar thereby getting the most value from them.

His patriotism is shown his mode of operation where all the major industries are here in Nigeria and African despite challenges of doing business here especially on power issues. Rather than exporting jobs that start from the assembling of these plants to produce and the cycle continues, he has domesticated all that here and more Nigerians are beneficiaries. He is proving that with grit, determination and going the long haul on any endeavour can guarantee success.

He is the true champion of make Nigerian and buys Nigerian. Yes, there are other Nigerian products that came about by the recent campaigns but most of which import their raw materials and produce here or produce abroad and brand it Nigerian. However, a Dangote is making sure to use the raw materials that God has blessed us with; he is tapping into them to the barest minimum without any issue of selling them raw. His products are local/Nigerian but today are regarded across Africa and in the Western world.

Aliko Dangote is a proud son of Africa and the world who is proving every day that it doesn't have to be white to be right. There is no dishonourable thing about being black and we can do that which the rest of the world can reckon with it.

He turned 60 this month and my prayer is that he will live long to create an impact that the next generation of business owners can learn from.

55.   WHAT SOUTH-EAST LEADERS NEED TO UNDERSTAND

Some truths in life don't need any explanation or a call to defend it rather proofs of such truths exist and can be found around us. Nigeria today is known to have an imbalanced federalism when judging by the modus operandi of it; many states and local government have feelings of marginalization; some have found a way to enlarge their territories so that allocations from the central government can come more to them.

Northern states are known for their landmass which also means more allocations for them while those that are down South feel that this is a good reason to agitate for marginalization. In as much as more monies might have gone to the Northern region when compared to what those in the South-Eastern States got, it doesn't justify an unfortunate situation where the development down south does not equate with the monies that have been disbursed over the years. Igbos are well known for their grit in merchandise, trade and buying and selling; come to Anambra state you will know that there are people who are wealthy by all standards. People, who in so many ways might have investments in the North and are doing well for themselves, family and kinsmen, unfortunately, the manner of politics by those who should manage the cake that comes from Abuja has been nothing but an abysmal failure.

How else can one justify the huge infrastructure deficit in the many South-Eastern States? How can Owerri (Imo state capital) that was built by Sam Mbakwe (with the same infrastructure) still be what we see today? What were all the monies used for, what industries or assets were built and what account can be credible to justify the state of our states in the South-East?

The political leaders from the South-Eastern region need to understand that the call of marginalization and secession is partly fueled by their non-performance; yes there is a structural deficit in Nigeria's federalism but that has not stopped allocations from coming in every month. The sharing formula and their naira equivalent are received by every state of the federation and our backwardness in infrastructure does not justify good appropriation. The activities of IPOB (Indigenous People of Biafra) seem justifiable because they feel people in Abuja are shortchanging us when we should be asking those who should be managing our wealth and resources.

Ever wondered why many Igbo merchants are scattered all over the North, is it that what they sell cannot be bought by their kit and kin in the East? The answer to that is quite obvious if we are to weigh the many options and factors that have our people sojourning in strange lands, home and abroad.

On the other hand, many of us have been clamouring for Igbo presidency and I ask, "Who do you want to send?" Good and fine we have great businessmen and those who call the shots in politics are either incompetent or clueless or big armed robbers. Igbos might be the third largest ethnic group in Nigeria but we are far from being the majority, so the rest of Nigeria will not rally behind someone who has not succeeded in his home state or in the greater Nigerian politics and beyond. Most of our governors (past and present) are the likely candidates that can vie for the office of the Presidency, but if there is no proof of their works in a state, how then can they handle the large, complicated entity known as Nigeria.

56.   A WAY OUT FOR DEVELOPING THE SOUTHEASTERN STATES

It is very embarrassing to hear a governor from one of the States complain of the national allocation not being enough when they are not the only states affected. The federalism Nigeria operates has not given full economic autonomy to the states and this applies to every state of the federation.

South-Easterners are made up of people who have through sheer grit, determination and leveraging latent opportunities to create good wealth for themselves. These can be found in all the five states in the region. What stops our political leaders and policymakers from creating a partnership with these private and individual businesses, with the aim of uplifting lives of our kit and kin, developing our states, rebuilding infrastructure, industrializing our region and creating collective wealth.

A visionary state governor with the right political will and determination can go a long way in initiating this relationship and partnership with the businessmen and women in his state. Once they see that you have a high goal of making the state better and that they were business people have something to gain; in money and fame, they will definitely cash in.

If the allocation from Abuja is not enough (not verified), then that is not a sentence to backwardness for the South-Eastern States; we can leverage our human capital and the power of the elite to build the region that we desire. We can show that merchandising can also be applied to state building and development. It is in doubt that there many wealthy Igbomen and women who in their nature prefer to cater for their immediate and extended family needs. No one feels obligated to contribute to the society especially when they don't find the government of the day being cooperative. Our political leaders need to move from holding on to the fort and take it further to moving it for the benefit of all people. We need to apply the skill of running our businesses in politics, governance and government. Joint ventures that will bring big shots in business and government will go a long way to drive inclusive growth and uplift the lives of our people. It will make the home more attractive, there won't be a need for so much sojourn outside our country homes unless for purposes of visiting and holidays.

Who says we can't have our own Lagos from any of our cities or a Dubai or even more than they have there. Nations like Singapore and the United Arab Emirates have proved that a nation can achieve true greatness even in the midst of high stake challenges, scarcity of resources and non-availability of minerals. The will and zeal of the people are enough; the need to survive, thrive and make something for ourselves is enough to push people to be creative and innovative. If Biafra at war could be so innovative as they were, then there is no limit to what the Igboman can achieve within their regions in a united Nigeria.

We are the strongest species in this country and it is not a good thing that our strengths are only shown in foreign lands while our own remain desolate.

57.   HOW NIGERIAN PARENTS ARE DRAWING US BACK AS A COUNTRY

What I am about to share with you might be seen as an irrelevant and inconsequential issue in Nigeria's quest to move forward and experience real growth like other counterpart nations but looking at actually and from various perspectives, you will have no option but to agree.

It is an age long belief and mindset that Nigeria has a unity problem but in the last few months, I have come to discover that we don't have a unity problem. Unity being a priority goal for development has put us backwards. You might agree but unity in any Nigerian equation evokes the notions of disunity. Other societies built their countries on universally acceptable values; the values of honour, integrity, social justice, equality before God and the law many others. For us, in Nigeria, we decided to choose unity. Unity to what end, if we come together (which we are already), what next? Today tribes are united to perpetuate the lot and good of their kit and kin while the more important aspect of uniting Nigeria is left to suffer. When our federalism is designed to fan the embers of tribe, religion and ethnicity, then you know we are going nowhere.

What Nigeria lacks is an understanding of each other, embracing our diversity for the right reasons (not for federal allocations). So we are a rich cultural society and this is evident in so many ways but for this piece, I will deal with marriages and the drama that surrounds it. It will interest you to know and realize that Nigerian parents play politics with the marriages. Unfortunately, they or many have succeeded in passing it down from generation to generation.

How can a nation that is in need of cohesion achieve it if we don't understand each other and a fundamental tool of understanding is through families built on marriages? This, of course, involves inter-ethnic marriages, a fusion of two or more cultures for a greater benefit. It will interest you to know that tribalism or what decided to create by ourselves confuses the political leadership in giving Nigeria a collective vision. I hear people make reference to what you call the Nigerian Dream and unity is top on the list. If a leadership is committed, the activities of those below the cadre or citizens end up making things very difficult. Every institution of Nigeria and their personnel are after tribe enthronement, preponderance and entitlement.

Now to this Marriage Issue

With the way many young Nigerians are brought up and the exposure to modernity, globalization, social media, intellectual discussions and more; being in love can and is always taking them beyond tribes, state, continent and country. The scope of falling in love has increased as people are not limited by a person's root but rather have chosen to stick to who the person has become. That sounds like all that really matters; who and what she or he is.

To many people's disappointments, there are people who are still deeply connected to traditions, values, cultures that our tribes and ethnic groups stand for. Apart from each group's identity of themselves, everyone also has perceived or assumed or observed or misconstrued identity of others. They could be true or not. Our parents or the other generation are the purveyors of such traditions and beliefs. Their won't be needing to go into what you think or our parents have us think of each other whether Hausa, Igbo or Yoruba. Every now and then, you find two beautiful young people, perfect and in love who cannot tie the knot due to the forces of perceptions and notions about others. Our parents, despite how educated they are, are quick to tag an entire state one republic due to the habit of one female banker that did not treat them like they wanted. Some people have even taken it to another level by playing tribal sentiments to political and social ambitions. The movie Wedding Party was beyond just tribe you know.

We have an opportunity to co-habit, co-create and co-procreate for the greater good of our country. Inter-tribal marriages can build trust, help us learn more of each other's traditions. We are quick to discern the bad ones from a distance but it is only when you draw closer that you will see the good in another. I challenge every entity in Nigeria that inter-marriage can work greater miracles in a shorter time than the NYSC scheme has achieved in over 40 years. The National Youth Service Corps brings people together for a time and after one year, everyone reverts back to their genesis, while inter-marriage can fuse families and whole generations together and a chain reaction of good news will keep erupting. Do you know how happy I am that I know a Remi Chinedu Ademiju? That is an everlasting union that death cannot part.

This might seem like child's play but it is serious like other issues in Nigeria. In fact, it is more serious than Dino's certificate. Singapore was match-making couples so that they can produce better children. Yes, you heard me right. You are to marry this kind of person for the sake of your children.

Fellow millennials, it is time to break free the Etisalat way, no better way to say it. The next 50 years of Nigeria and the journey to our century of independence is in our hands and if we must be better than the passing generation, we must fix this issue. Our greatness is tied to understanding each other. There is nothing wrong in Emeka understanding what happens in Yorubaland or any other of 200 ethnic groups. There is nothing also wrong if Bello is well grounded in Igbo culture. I had a Sa'ed Abdulmajid who knew how to speak Igbo in my class in secondary school (high school).

Our economic, social and political changes (for good) are all tied to our cultural change (for good).

Support Inter-Marriage.

58.   THE LANGUAGE OF NATION BUILDING

And the Lord said, Behold, the people is one, and they have all one language; and this they begin to do: and now nothing will be restrained from them which they imagined doing.

1:6

The above scriptural passage talks about the men who were involved in the construction of the Tower of Babel that would have been the tallest structure built by man in history. Their goal was to get to heaven; God's throne and God himself acknowledged the following about that particular generation;

- ✓ The people were one. Oneness connotes cooperation, synergy, concerted efforts, collective energy, and unity.
- ✓ They all had one language. This can mean speaking the language but can also be said to be about communication; they understood each other, the same vision, mindset, the possibility mentality of attaining anything was evident in every one of them. In essence, they had a common ground of understanding.
- ✓ They pursue collectively as one nation and one people. Everyone was part of the building process and no one was found working against the process.
- ✓ Then there was a power of imagination that was fueled by curiosity. They were asking obviously

asking questions about how heaven was, how God's throne was like and this they wanted to satisfy by imagining a tower that would go up to heaven.

The above illustrations took me down memory lane of how the United Arab Emirates was able to transform a desert nation into one that is filled with many architectural masterpieces that touch the sky. If you have seen the documentary on the birthing of the idea of Burj Al Rab, you will understand why I am making reference to this nation that is transforming architecture and construction simply by having an idea. How their leaders were able to rally citizen support to build something that will be a world record. That is not child's play.

The challenge of many developing nations of today is their inability or those of their leaders to inspire collective visions, goals and hope for the people. Democracy is even making it more difficult as everyone thinks he has the idea and better plan to make things work. Singapore, a success story any day, though, a democracy was built on the vision of their founding father, Lee Kuan Yew and he was authoritative when he needed to. He was a leader by all standards and one unique quality of this man was that he saw problems and challenges before anyone else and set out to solve them. The government under him never waited for a problem to degenerate badly before a solution is thought out.

If the leaders in African can succeed in rallying their different nations into a just, humane, honest and worthy cause of rebuilding their nations the right way, then we would surprise the world. Nigeria for instance, asides the existence of diversity in her culture, is filled with vested and special interest groups in almost every sector. More people are daily concerned about how only them and their families can get better. The extent of our free economic system or capitalism is more like war; we are on a battlefield of survival and most strategies are to kill the competition.

Nations that experience rapid growth are the ones that work together, those that break down every wall of division, countries that embrace diversity as a strength rather than as an avenue to reap off one another and harness the power of cohesion, synergy, common purpose and the same mindset to build individually and as a nation.

59.   NIGERIA AND OUR POTS OF PORRIDGE

The biblical story of Jacob and Isaac tells us of how Esau out of hunger (which was temporary) sold his birthright to a Jacob who probably knew the benefit of what Esau was about to let go with just a plate of porridge. As much as that was an inconsequential exchange between two brothers, we eventually knew that he lost a blessing that was due to him by that very harmless act.

A major occurrence in the socio-economic and political sphere of Nigeria is that some people behind the scene mobilize young people or otherwise to stage different kinds of protests across the country. Political campaigns and rallies are thronged by crowds that have been paid to make it look like candidates have the people's support. No wonder they are too confident they cannot lose the election; because they feel they have bought Nigerians over, don't want to lose their investment or maybe something more.

The rent a crowd syndrome is becoming part of our national identity, some people are out to exploit the desperation of Nigeria (for economic needs) in corrupting the fabric of our political, social and economic journey. At the polls, many don't blink an eyelid to vote for a fool criminal for a meagre sum of a thousand five hundred, and this, of course, is for obvious reasons that seem justifiable in their eyes.

More recently, we hear that some people decided to protest against Amnesty International for their report against the Nigerian Army for human rights abuses. It is in this same country and in this same month (of March) that clips of soldiers beating up civilians were seen on the internet yet, some people are staging a protest against an organization that filed a report against it. As much as we want to protect our national integrity, I wonder what could be more damning to our reputation that we have to pay a crowd of people to protest against issues that false and unfounded.

We are, without knowing selling out our birthright; we are mortgaging our future by allowing a few vested interests buy over the uneducated and downtrodden among us. They are being offered pots of porridge that are worth about two thousand naira and this is making the uneducated voiceless seeing that a large percentage are in abject poverty. Polling booths during elections are more occupied by the poor in the society who come out with the hope that one thief of a politician can offer a thousand or two for their votes and franchise to be bought over.

This trend is beginning to take root and more uneducated and unenlightened are buying because they have to feed and make ends meet. To them, it is nothing so long as they are able to get some cash simply by doing what is expected by those renting them. It is up to the educated ones among us (Nigerians) to rise up and do something about this, these people who are selling unworthy causes to a few of us need to be stopped so that the serious won't be neglected because there is no fee on it.

Let us not mortgage our blessings and path us progress by allowing a few people who only have access to money deny us of what truly is noble, dignified and worthy.

60.   IT ISN'T JUST SUICIDE, THERE IS MORE...

As more people take personal responsibility to take their lives, reactions have trailed what could be the cause of such unfortunate act. Most think it is the recession that has sparked lots of downward, downcast, depressing trends in the country. People have obviously gotten to break point and can no longer pull through or keep their endurance and perseverance in check. We are almost in a state of anarchy but God forbid that unfortunate act continues and may we come out stronger at the end of it all.

But guess what? This shit is beyond suicide, there is more to it, there is more to what the recession is unleashing, there is more to what it is making Nigerians do and everyone is reacting differently. The good part of all these reactions is that some are good and great even as more people are becoming more creative and innovative. The economic woes have forced people to retreat, rethink, restrategize and also rediscover themselves. That's a blessing if you ask me.

Then to the rest, what I call the social effects of recession; character, attitudes are being affected directly and indirectly. Have you come across two motorists who by their own making or carelessly hit themselves or one hits another; you will some talking calmly from their car, they start raising their voices and then progress to walk out their car (in a moving traffic into and estate). At this point, it won't be wrong to assume that within the time of speaking from the car to coming out and start venting, there was a thought of the money it will take to repair the car. People become hostility induced by a thought of the fact that another person is trying to make them spend money in an economy of recession. That's not funny!

Money has come to understand can induce different kind of emotions; which can come in two different situations; when you have it and don't have it. The reason why the good says that the love of money is the root of all evil is that when it gets to the point of men becoming emotionally attached to it, then unfortunate things can be done for it; in times of abundance or lack. When the emotions like we all do start getting involved, the brain and mind lose their value and influence.

That is why when a man loses money he acts the exact opposite of what he does when it comes in; excitement or grief. This is so because they have refused to see money as a means to an end rather than being the end of life or purpose or why we are here.

So in this recession that seems to be affecting different people differently, we are bound to have different reactions; of creativity, innovation, rashness, frustration, anger, hate, despair, hope, etc. Whatever one chooses to do with what is happening now all depends on their perception of life and happiness.

61.   THE BOYCOTT ATTITUDE OF NIGERIANS

In the news some time ago was the outcry of the Comptroller General of Customs about how they won't be able to meet their 1 trillion naira target for 2017. He, however, attributed this to the activities of smugglers at different entry points into the country. Last year, 2016, had them making about 890 billion which is below the set target of 1 trillion naira.

One would ask why Nigerians find it difficult to pay their rent in the rent-seeking economy we have. Isn't it just about 10-15 % VAT or import duties?

Also, I have seen people decide to change direction while driving especially when they sight either Road Safety or

VIO officials. Yes, obviously their papers might not be complete but why will one choose not to do the needful for the various vehicle registrations needed?

Government is quick to advertise or advice us to pay tax but how do they expect us to react when the roads to many estates in Abuja are in deplorable states? We have a huge infrastructure deficit, yet taxes are collected in billions every year. Nigerians boycotting various taxes and levies isn't just about the amount involved but because of a loss of confidence on how these monies are appropriated for all our benefits. There is no justification for public schools, hospitals and various government-managed facilities that huge sums are being remitted by hardworking Nigerians.

There are people making so much in a month/year but when the time comes to pay tax, they file for bankruptcy. A person who burns diesel to run his business, what rationale does he have to pay tax/levies that can't fix the power problems that will, in turn, help his business.

A people don't just set out to be law breakers or tax evaders, there is always a precedent to every action or counter-action by Nigerians. People feel withdrawn and exonerated from their government. The manner and approach through which the paramilitary officers and government officials try to extort money from private citizens are alarming. I can remember one who followed me to the ATM to get cash for supposed traffic disobedience.

The Responsibility of Government

The Buhari government might have a lot of goodwill but they still need to prove it in deeds, action, communication, connection, through facts, figures and data. Thank God for the Freedom of Information (FOI) bill, Nigerians need to be aware of how money comes in and how they are appropriated, spent and used to execute projects.

For a people that have lost a great deal of confidence in governance for many years, any government that desires change must go to the extreme to win it back. The government must do what has never been done before, they must grant the people access both online and offline. Not many Nigerians understand how Twitter works or the engagements that go on there, these ones need to be reached using a different approach that suits them.

Loss of confidence in governance and government has some dire consequences. Most of all, the citizens will hardly offer their cooperation in policy matters and programs even though such policy might be laudable. They will see it as the same old order they have been used to. Good ideas die natural deaths because citizens don't buy into it or their hopes of many years have been dashed by many failures of those in power. So, all political leaders are all tagged as one republic.

Finally, Customs Comptroller General might have issued an order to his people to take their supervisory roles seriously but if the government fails to convince the so-called smugglers and businessmen/women why and where their monies are being used, then it will all be an effort in futility. The smuggling and other forms of boycott will continue and for how long? So, is not about the money/tax to be paid but on what it has been used for in times past.

62. WHAT MAKES @OMOJUWA, @AYOURB, @MRFIXNIGERIA, @TOYOSIRISE, @RENOOMOKRI, @DEMOLAREWAJU, @FUNMILOLA, @AYOSOGUNRO

@OGUNDAMISI @BLOSSOMOZURUMBA AND CO. DIFFERENT FROM EACH OTHER?

Before I delve into what I want to drive home with this title that seems controversial and obviously lengthy, let me say that the people mentioned above are those I respect so much and I am fond of visiting their pages or twitter handles to know what they are up to. That has been my way of learning from them if I can't get direct access.

These people have a lot in common, they are young people who I would say are part of the fifth generation of leaders that Nigeria will have, they are enlightened about Nigeria's socio-political issues, they desire a change for our country and in their own personal spaces have also blazed the trail. They are not regarded as twitter celebrities because of the number of followers but for the good influence, they command among those who admire them.

On the one thing they have in common; Nigeria, her politics, our journey and a desire to change and achieve true greatness. I really don't know the reason why they tend to disagree on Nigerian politics, why they have to call out on each other and always in disagreement. The leaders that you all defend whether as GEJites or Buharists or APC or PDP or you simply are standing alone don't disagree on real issues. Serious issues like federalism or our structural formation as a country are not even in the founding documents of these political parties you all support. All we hear are a Buhari's certificate or that of Dino Melaye. Trump might be shaking up the world but as a Republican, we know where he stands and Obama as a Democrat also has a standing.

If you call a Republican today and a Democrat, their stance on national issues are almost predictable; longstanding values and philosophies.

The run-up to the 2015 elections was the height of it all, many twitter fights or arguments or the program (PLAY Forum) that was anchored by Tolu Ogunlesi where young APC and PDP youths where almost getting physical in Transcorp Hilton till around 12:30 am. You all argue, debate and take on each other but never on any real issue, which of you supports true federalism, PDP or APC?

So in all of this, all I see is an egoistic fight of personal opinions or convictions. Each of you most of the time are right about your views on how Nigeria can move forward, so why the choice of being in different camps when you all want the same thing; a better Nigeria. If you were disagreeing on philosophies or matters of principles or national issues that would be understandable but right now you are not.

So why do you think the best thing for this generation is for us to be divided under the old generation who have glaringly failed Nigeria in their own half a century of leadership. The next remaining half of our journey to a century of independence has started and it is our generation that will be involved in it. Are we going to go the way of our fathers or we would chart a better course for our time? You are the ones with a loud voice in this generation and you have a greater advantage of uniting us against the enemies of the Nigerian state. If you must disagree, let it be on real issues, economic issues, structural issues of our federalism, on crime, etc, and not on Dino's certificate, please.

If you are not aware many Nigerians look up to you and if you are a fighter today, many millennials of today expect you to be a fighter tomorrow on real issues in the polity. The standards are being set and you are lifting every day in your tweets and in the near future reference will be made to them. You will be asked to defend this tweet and that tweet.

You all are divided and disagreeing when in actual sense you want the same thing for our country. You want probity, social justice, sanity in the minds of Nigerians, rule of law, creativity and innovation in government and more. So an Omojuwa wants the same thing as Ohimai, that Nigeria achieves her true potential. Please, you all need to close ranks, unite this generation for the right reasons, and when politics comes let it be done on things that matter.

Like Aunty Oby has been saying for quite some time, "we have an urgency of now" (she alone knows what she sees and the reason for the emphasis) but it falls to this generation to decide "what the urgency of how is".

You all are the leaders of this generation!

63.   YOUNG NIGERIANS: LEARN FROM MAJOR NZEOGWU

For the purpose of clarity of history, Major Chukwuma Kaduna Nzeogwu is an Okpanam man (present day Delta State) who is known to have participated in the maiden coup in Nigeria on January 15th, 1966. That day is still observed as Armed Forces Remembrance Day in Nigeria. Like many still think, Major Nzeogwu was not the leader of the coup but because the territory (Kaduna State, Northern Nigeria) which he controlled was successfully executed with the unfortunate killing of Sardauna and Belewa, he has been seen by many as the lead coup plotter. The leader of the coup was Major Emmanual Ifeajuna who was stationed to take out the South (precisely Lagos) but as was his nature has been from high school, he abandoned his mission halfway reneged.

So the lead hero or villain of that day remains Major Nzeogwu though there were many other players. The events of that day changed the course of Nigerian history and ushered us into wars of guns, matchets, words and every weapon of destruction. However, the man thought he was doing us and Nigeria a favour, by opting for violence to sack a government that was barely 6 years after independence but already wallowing in corruption. The argument of whether Chukwuma Nzeogwu was a hero or villain can practically shut down Nigerian Twitter space and even start offline fights. Whichever the case, there is still lesson to learn by this generation from this Major whose name has been engraved in our political history forever.

Who was the man?

Nzeogwu was like every other young Nigeria who today is on social media or otherwise that keeps talking about Nigeria, our journey and challenges; the difference is that his own space was in the army barracks, officers' mess, in the war front in Congo and some political gatherings as well. He never hid his frustration about the shortcomings of others, a disciplined man, non-alcoholic, was not a womanizer, committed to his duties as a Nigerian officer, was frustrated with the treatment of blacks in the Congo while whites enjoyed in our land and he surely talked about the potential of Nigeria. The man was politically aware despite being an officer. Soldiers were believed to be apolitical or are not supposed to be involved in politics but rather safeguard the nation from external aggression or implosion.

Let me add therefore that the coup of that day was not for any of the Majors to assume political power but was to release Chief Obafemi Awolowo who was in Prison (in Calabar) for treason, form a presidential commission of Army officers and install Awo as President. That information might make us rethink the notion that it was an Igbo coup to perpetuate the powers of the Igbo race.

Chukwuma never spoke from just opinions or commonsense, the man was studious, he read books and was knowledgeable on what applies elsewhere and how other nations have moved forward. In preparation for the big day he studied, read books on Marshall Tito and guerrilla activities in Yugoslavia in the Nazi era. In essence, he prepared for whatever he was planning, a coup or revolution and the reasons were genuine; to stop the corruption in government by changing it. Though the means to attain was not humane, they were acting on what they thought was right and maybe how it has been achieved in some other nations.

The days leading up to Exercise Damisa and January 15 had a lot of planning go into it and was of course executed under the leadership of Major Nzeogwu. Now, this in no way is the justification for the killing of Sardauna, Belewa, Brig. Ademulegun and others; just to show that these young officers had a desire for a change in their country, developed a plan, followed through and executed it. They were the young people of that generation who by virtue of military power felt they could leverage on that to change things. Chukwuma Kaduna Nzeogwu might be hated by some for obvious reasons but the end of what that exercise was to achieve was genuine and patriotic but the means has made him a villain and cause of the problems that led up to a civil war and subsequent national problems.

Now to Young Nigerians of Today

We are now in a democratic setting which does not mean that change cannot happen or that a government cannot be deposed through democratic means. By all indications, the old order of Nigerian leaders has not had a distinction in handling our affairs. Yes, there are successes but they are not enough to keep us on par with those we started the journey with us. Not close enough! It is also unfortunate and disheartening that they seem to be doing things that are wrong even to a 5-year old, the graft is high, we are being trampled upon, human dignity is at the lowest ebb yet we are not moving forward fast enough. A greater challenge is that most Nigerians have lost hope in their government, in Nigeria and every framework that makes us one; that means that the next generation of leaders have a greater work of trust rebuilding and regaining the confidence of citizens in their own country.

How then are the next generation preparing, what plans we have, what measures, timeline and more? The majors chose January 15, 1966. What even is our plan for 2019? Whether we like it or not, this old order is eating up on our part of the century and is not ready to relinquish power or give us the opportunity to play our part.

We think tweeting and social media bants can do anything on the ground or win elections. If Nzeogwu is somewhere looking at us, he will see us as jokers. Yes, we are not in a military era to start wielding guns and tanks, yet there are democratic tools to take back our country. We are simply utilizing the latest of them, social media which those in power are even trying to phase out and make unlawful. So I guess that plan failed but they can afford to take the twitter heat and endure while they do their evil. *For Dino to come and dance for you and tell you ntooo (tongue out), you know that he feels safe because our sting don't even touch his skin.*

If we are going to take back our nation, we need to do more than banter and fight with each other on Twitter; those are small battles. The wars that will see us save our country are way beyond that and are not fought at the comfort of your room/ office or closets. Ask Nelson Mandela! He too had to create an army to face a system that was being violent to his people. **You need to approach the enemy with the same tool of war or something more superior.**

What must we do?

So you don't go and misquote me or my reference to history, taking back our country will involve these and not limited to these;

1. We need to have a goal, a plan, timeline for achievement and the strategies to achieve them. We understand democracy and should also understand the mechanisms of operation; whether a political party or whatever.

2. Of high importance is that we must gain knowledge, study, acquire skills, and build competence not to install others alone (like the Majors) but also participate in politics and governance.

3. In this era of politics and democracy, one must build wealth the right way. In acquiring skills it must be to create value for others and ourselves. The wealth can be collectively created because if we are to confront these ones, we need plenty of it and of course it must be legitimate so we don't repeat the wrongs we are trying to correct.

4. We need to close ranks and stop the unnecessary fights on twitter especially by those who have a loud voice among us. I really don't know why they disagree; on what issues but on baseless things like girlfriends, relationships and Dino's certificate. What happens to power, job creation, federalism, state police, etc? We need to get serious.

5. We need to focus on issues that will make us more relevant than those holding siege on us. We need to offer better solutions and create more and real value.

I don't know why I have been making reference to what Aunty Oby Ezekwesili has been saying for some time now, "We have an urgency of now!" The truth in this cannot be overemphasized and I am sure she has her unique reasons for saying that but whichever the case, it is the job of the young generation to decide what the "urgency of how" will be. *It is good to realize that there is an urgency of now but real rewards will come when we figure out how to change.*

May we be wise enough to know how to go into the city.

64.   IF FEMINISM & GENDER EQUALITY MUST BE REALIZED

The concept of feminism and gender equality is gaining ground every day. More individuals, organizations, states and nations are showing their support for the female folks especially with the many prejudices they are faced with. More voices are rising to speak for the female folks both male and female and on my part, I have decided to call myself a selective feminist. Like it or not, I would love to have my daughters treated with dignity, respect wherever they find themselves. Likewise, I will teach my sons to respect every woman they come across in their lifetime.

A feminist is seen as someone who believes in the social, political and economic equality of the sexes. They desire to be treated with respect, the desire more economic opportunities because they can create same value like their male counterparts. A woman was close to being the leader of the free world and that further gave the womenfolk a stronger voice. It's not in doubt that women have proved their worth in business, politics, arts, science and in virtually every sphere of life.

We celebrated this year's International Women's Day in March and many people shared their views for women. A major issue that comes to be bear was on domestic and sexual violence and by all standards; hitting or violating a woman is not justifiable. Based on the movie Fireproof, we are told that a woman is like a flower, if you treat her right she will bloom, if you don't she will wilt. I have come to understand that no matter how unbearing, crazy or difficult any woman can be, she can be tamed, her sweetness can be drawn out, her best moment and part is within; it requires the right person to draw it out. Feminists can be defensive, can try to match up with men but it also takes the right man to gain access to the woman in every feminist.

Feminism for me is not complete without the virtues that every woman is expected to have. The substance is key, content is priceless, the value is invaluable. There is nothing that inspires a man like a woman that embodies all these. It helps a man in business and career. Napoleon Hill in his book, Think and Grow Rich calls it the mystery of sex transmutation. A success secret that is made possible by a connection with someone of the opposite sex. Let me add that many such women are in abundance in the society.

Yet!

There is still a good measure of women who are lacking in value. Women who make a god of their bodies while the inner woman is bereft of any form of substance. Social media today has handles (on Twitter) that use nude, semi-nude pictures to showcase social marketing of all kinds. In as much as these people might be creating value, the object of attraction/logo is the flaunting of their boobs and other body parts. I think every woman has an element of nudity (not necessarily explicit), but that nature of flaunting their bodies in beautiful clothes and accessories. However, many people have taken it to a point of seduction to be able to market their value. Can't the value of products and services speak for themselves without a revealing of body parts?

The kind of feminism that can be beneficial to our society is one that is targeted at increasing the self-esteem of women when it comes to the male counterpart or in the society. Men generally need women in their lives, they need to satisfy their sexual desires, and they need someone to help organize their lives, home and business. The role of women in the lives of men has been proven since the creation of man and many contemporary stories exist to back this up. Men need women to procreate their name and generation, a woman can inspire you; give you the push needed to achieve greatness.

Unfortunately, today, not all women or ladies out there understand this. Young ladies are exposed wrongly; they inculcate the worst of mindsets that end up leaving them treated like rags in the hands of men. It is also disheartening that young ladies still think that sex can be used to gain his respect or that the body tool and influence still works magic. It can work momentarily but men desire something more eternal and sustainable.

Feminism is not a bad concept or phenomenon but it will be better for those who have discovered their worth as women to help others who have not to do same. There are many wrong notions about sexuality, relationships and love it is high time they are corrected. They must be corrected in the minds of many young ladies out there.

The Business of Politics

I received a tweet update on my regarding a partnership between Nigerian governors, Bill Gates, Dangote Foundation and the UK government in an effort to produce vaccines across the nation. That tweet prompted me to write this piece to drive a point or a quick observation. That's how inspiration can come for me but one must be willing and ready to put that second of thought into a well-developed piece.

It is common knowledge that business leaders are business leaders while politicians are political leaders i.e. their main and only focus is governance and governmental issues that will most times involve policy-making and drafting of laws. It is worthy mandate to have a government doing all these because we need a sane, disciplined society where rules guide or actions and inaction as a people. These laws go further to address issues in the business and financial sectors. You can say the government is giving the direction and the compass of our development.

What if the government can expand their scope of operation aside just making laws or dealing with the public and civil servants? A government that can set up a business venture targeted at creating jobs, engaging her people, make profits from within and without and use this same profit for developmental projects and programs. It sounds more like having a system sustaining itself and the money circulating and multiplying domestically.

For instance, this has been implemented in the transport industry that was mostly dominated by private businesses. We started having state-owned transport companies; Imo Transport Company (ITC), Rivers Transport Company (RTC), Transport Company of Anambra State (TRACAS), Benue Line, Abia Line, etc. These ventures can be managed by private individuals employed by the government, given targets to operate and make profits as a business and also able to scale up as much as their innovation allows. This can also be implemented in a state that is rich in rubber trees that can be used in producing rubber-related products in footwears, tyres, etc.

This style of governance was highly adopted Singapore and their story to a first world nation. Housing corporations were set up to meet the needs and demands of housing deficit also aimed at making it possible for the citizens to acquire their own homes and resale if they so desire. This style must not be limited to available raw materials but can work with the importation of technology and attraction of Foreign Direct Investment (FDI).

This same method can be adopted in the solid minerals ministry as they plan to go into full-scale mining. Rather than make it a federal affair like the Oil industry, it will necessary to decentralize the processes of mining so that state governments can handle it, remit a percentage that can be used to develop areas that don't have any natural resources.

Governments should be run as businesses that can create value for the people and also generate funds internally and externally for other developmental projects and programs.

65.   THE MYSTERY OF ONE MAN

Can a Tree Make a Forest?

The above question has been used in an adage that says, "a tree cannot make a forest", and this, in fact, has been the mindset of those who have looked at it literarily as it appears. One tree to them is not enough to create a mighty forest of other trees, but is that entirely true?

What is the nature of a tree that is expected to bear fruits by the way?

If a single tree is planted, nurtured, watered and managed to grow into a full tree with fruits all over its leaves and branches. With external factors like the wind beating on this particular tree, some of its fruits will have to drop and scattered at the bottom of the tree, far and near. In no time those fruits will germinate too and become trees of their own and this process is allowed and permitted to continue until a forest is formed. Don't forget the first tree will have its fruits scattered in certain directions and distance and the ones that follow will also follow suit until a considerable size of a forest is formed.

The above process is a natural one and can be explained without having to be diminished by the initial quote that "a tree cannot make a forest".

When you compare a tree to a man that has seeds, ideas, vision, knowledge, imagination, faith, courage, wisdom, power and every other good virtue one can think of, you can agree with me that one man can actually accomplish great things. In biblical times, when God decides to call his people out, save them, or deliver them from the hands of the oppressor he sends a man. He equips one person who will be the leader of that generation, who will communicate His will, who will chart the course of the future for the nation of Israel. That has always been the strategy God adopts and it has never failed in achieving success unless the man fails himself.

These personalities who are called to bear a new message for God's people can be seen in Noah, Abraham, Jacob, Nehemiah, Samson, Gideon, Esther, David, Solomon, Samuel, Jesus and many more. Contemporary times is also littered with people who at one point in history and human civilization played a major role in making the world a better place by the enormity of a vision they had. Vision is received, given or inspired by circumstances that one sees around; key factor is that it is always given to individuals, not groups. The individual will definitely to sell his vision to other people who are allowed to work in fulfilling it but the passion, determination and the knowledge the visionary has is key to bringing it to fruition.

This book was inspired by the story of Gideon in the Bible where God called him out to deliver the Israelites from the hand of the Midianites who were holding them captive. In the book of Judges where this story was captured, we are told that Gideon was not confident about his capabilities to be the deliverer of Israel; his roots bothered him that he felt unqualified. And of course in the sixteenth verse of the sixth chapter God said to Gideon; "Surely I will be with you, and you shall defeat the Midianites as *one man*".

I concluded in my mind that there is a mystery behind one man; a man with vision, a man of purpose, a man with ideas, a man with power, a man that is knowledgeable and a man that is charged and fully equipped.

66.   UNDERSTANDING HOW POLITICS AFFECTS YOU

After many months of deliberations, several meetings and consultations with constituent members of government and the people, the Commander-In-Chief realizing that the Armed Forces was short personnel issued a and Executive order that every male above the age of 21 and less than 45 years be recruited into the military for the next phase of war against our enemies in battle. The battle to ensure territorial integrity, and equally, keep the resources of the threatened territories under siege.

Recruitment will be immediate without many bureaucratic processes; once you are verified to be over 21 years of age your enlistment is automatic and expected to resume with 3 days. This order had some families have their children (all male) to be drafted into a war that will be our greatest mistake in history.

"Patriots, the commandant screamed, "your training should be seen as a preparation and equipping to show the love for your country and it will run for 3 weeks after which you will be empowered to wield a rifle and be in control and total control of the triggers." Understood?

"Sir, Yes Sir," the new recruits responded, some feeling proud and some other not sure of how they really feel while some were scared.

That is the power those in power hold; to make laws, pass decrees, and cooperate in a bid to make themselves safer while the rest of citizens are to ensure that safety. The power to do great good and untold evil is in their hands; they can wield it like monsters or saints and at the end, the resultant effect is on all those regarded as the common man or citizens. If you either excited at politics, the drama and gaming involved or you are indifferent or you are simply cowed to fear and intimation; either of these categories does not guarantee your safety. In fact, you become more vulnerable like those young soldiers who outside their choices are going to pay the ultimate prices for the mistakes of clueless men and women in government.

The war for the soul of any nation; whether internal war, election wars, tribal wars, religious wars have those in power issuing orders for the children of other people to execute while theirs remain in safe havens funded by the people. They will tell you to do this for love of country, to defend your country, to be a patriot for their bad, distasteful wrong decisions and choices. All these are in an efforts to brainwash you, make you see good in a glaring evil and make you feel good about your actions to justify theirs.

Hello; wake up!

Power (politics), Money and Influence all have the power to do two things; good or evil. There is no mid-point to it. Any other embellishments for reasons are to make you see either good or evil against yourself without even knowing sometimes. You either defend your rights or guarantee for safety or you remain laid back for the worst to come upon you.

67.   NIGERIA AS A ZOO: AN IDEAL DESCRIPTION

The description of Nigeria as a zoo was first echoed by the leader of the Indigenous People of Biafra (IPOB), Mazi Nnamdi Kanu while he was still canvassing for the breakaway of the defunct Biafran Republic from Nigerian territories. That created a lot of controversies, counter reactions and of course, as it is the nature of Nigeria lots of jokes, memes and laughs about it.

The zoo name equally received a statement by a seating Senator from Kaduna State, Shehu Sani and a followed up mention by the Wife of the President, Aisha Buhari. Zoo takes up one back to the book by George Orwell Animal Farm, I will try as much as possible to decipher what the correlation is between the present day Nigeria and a typical zoo anywhere in the world.

Firstly, a zoo is largely created artificially because you can compare it the evil forest that is known in Igboland. So humans like the British come together and create a zoo of various species and ethnicity. They have different ways of life, believe in different things, eat different things, have different ways of survival and of course, this differences created friction and preying on one another. If a lion as the king of the jungle needs to survive, eat and feed fat, it means that a deer dares not cross its path. The first sight of each other will result in running away in different directions and in Nigeria, there is this siege mentality that a section of people have when they see others. You have to shiver when a cough let alone cross your path or you pay obeisance.

Secondly, the conservationists might create sections for different animals so that everyone can survive and live in harmony but of course, animals will always stray and be animals. Rules are made for our good living but citizens and people who should be living by it see it as normal to break such rules. They negate consequences that come individually or collectively and abuse laws, principles and at the end what you find is that things work differently here. Efforts cannot be directly promotional to rewards because rules of engagement will be broken to have such successes. I have seen people abuse the noblest of principles and give credit to God for it; what? This our God is indeed merciful!

Thirdly, a zoo is not for the fainthearted who walk gently when they see an animal that can prey on them. You have to become aggressive in your unique way to survive. You thrive based on survival instincts and approach or else you go into extinction. So, at the day of the day what we have is a fight against each other, bruises, scars, pains that we inflict on each because each one wants to rule and do so perpetually like Mugabe and the ones we have that share same mindsets even citizens   (outside of power).

Fourthly, a zoo is such that wealth is distributed unevenly. If you won't fight well enough or play by the immoral rules you are more or less dead. Those who scavenge for survival do so because the ones at the top of the food chain grab everything and refuse to even give the lower ones any crumbs. The higher animals ensure this and equally do well to keep the lower ones in check. You can have access to their growth instinct, the education is limited, the access is terrible and this they ensure in order for the common animals to generational slaves.

And finally, over time the lower animals might start learning to adapt, learn a few secrets of the higher ones. While the rich try to subdue the poor, the poor works their way behind the scene to challenges those who should be their fellow zoo citizens to a battle. They keep planning, strategizing, learning, unlearning old ways, learning new ways and relearning them for the sake of mastery. At this point, knowledge is built, education is acquired, Zimbabweans become aware and strengthened to challenge their Mugabe and at the appointed; they revolt.

The wives will revolt against any form of marriage or reason to be called fellow citizens with those who oppress them. This is the breaking point for the nation, this when things start getting out of hand, chaos is in the land, people are running and some others are committed to fighting until the end.

68. THE REAL INFLUENCE OF NIGERIA'S FEDERALISM

Nigeria as an independent, sovereign and democratic federal republic runs a federalism that has necessitated incessant calls for restructuring and review. The central government has been known to hold so much power over what is now regarded as the exclusive legislative list with about items under the purview of the federal government in Abuja, the federal capital territory. The content of this list includes economic, social and political sectors of the economy; so the states have no power to interfere or intervene in such matters under the law.

The economic aspect equally limits the state in meeting basic needs of her citizens and indigenes even for the payment of salaries, pensions and other overhead costs. Internally Generated Revenues can't do much to even purse programs, projects and create real impact for the people or even create a decent environment. To buttress this, each state receives a federal allocation to pursue programs as they wish without the central government in Abuja understanding fully of the happenings in the states. So, even when the population of a state like Imo state in the South-Eastern part of the country, they still receive the same percentage as stipulated in the sharing formula.

I have seen our Presidents unveiled programs in Abuja for the states like in education but the real picture of that is that the federal government blows a wind or send a ray of sunlight or hope from Abuja but as they proceed towards the states they diminish in impact and influence. Nigeria's federalism is such that economic policies, ideas, programs and initiatives of government never get the real impact particularly those by the federal/central government. Education which happens to be on the exclusive list or matters of mineral resources receives no real impetus in the hinterlands and rural areas because the offices presiding over them are all in Abuja.

A president of Nigeria breathes a breath of fresh air in Abuja but before it even gets far to touch or impact lives; it brings dust, heat or sadness or nothing to the people. The influence of Abuja over the vast territories of Nigeria is little, unfelt and trace in nature. Even within the boundaries of the FCT, there are places that don't receive government attention or presence; no good roads, hospitals or basic necessities for people to get by comfortably as bonafide citizens. The satellite towns of Lugbe, FHA and Bwari and many others are proofs to this.

What more can you say of places far in the north or down south in the creeks of the Niger Delta or the inner villages of Imo, Osun, Kwara, Niger, Benue, Plateau and other states of the federation?

In what do Nigerians feel the impact of their president and Commander-in-chief from Abuja?

In events like Lafia Doule, Python dances, Odi massacre, Zaki Ibiam and the deployment of the military or security operatives during elections to grab more power. When it comes to controlling violence that is caused by bad governance, you feel or government with the presence of soldiers who simply obey orders. How can we leave the matters of economic progress in Abuja with no influence down south or north yet the presence of the military can make world news in Aljazeera or CNN? What kind of federalism prioritizes military might and strength over economic opportunities and real empowerment to succeed?

Nigeria's history is characterized by patches of violence, killings, wars and what have you but when you look closely, you will find that our leaders and their stewardship in office led to these sad and unfortunate occurrences. The Army has no business interrupting political and democratic processes if things are done humanely and as it should. They are humans, they have families, children in civic schools and relatives who they care about. The leadership should take the blame for every reaction from citizens who are frustrated when they understand the true potential of their country and what we can achieve and how far other countries have gone.

The failure of Nigeria is a foundational and fundamental one of a constitution that does not create room for productivity, equity, wealth creation or to even dream as citizens, groups or collectively as one country. The system needs to be redesigned, the system needs a review, the system requires renegotiation, and the system needs a rebirth and revival.

We have no Nigerian problem, citizen issue, character flaw; the fundamental and underlying issue or flaw if there are any and of course, there are is the flaw of our constitution and the laws that still keep us one as Nigerians. Nigerians are worthy of character both home and abroad. What we seek is simply an opportunity to thrive as humans, thinkers, idealists, inventors, innovators, entrepreneurs, social entrepreneurs and total creatives.

69.   UNDERSTAND HOW POLITICS CAN AFFECT YOU (2)

We were in that traffic at Berger and wondering what was causing this unusual delay at 8:30 pm on a Monday morning. I tried manoeuvring my way without being scratched by these cab drivers that have no patience for any other road user. I couldn't go back to initiate a good turning radius without my bumper getting stained by the green on this green coloured taxis but thank God, my Golf was able to fit in. With that, I was able to get to the front and at that point, it dawned on me that some mobile policemen had blocked the right stretch of the roundabout and forcing everyone to fit in on the left.

"How can these ones are here tonight", I asked my tired self. Oh, a political party just had their convention (politics) and some security personnel were deployed for their protection (for just convention). And at 8:30 pm they were still under instruction to keep checking citizens who are eager to go home and rest after a long day and the first day of the week. I guess they have chosen their leaders and now as the election year draws nearer, one can imagine how many roads will be blocked on the campaign trail.

Did they even consult the public on the choice of their party leaders, who knows them and with the way many are jostling to occupy many few seats like the Party chairman, one wonders what vision all these contenders have different from each other? Whoever gets elected will play a major role for the next round of elections and of course, the consequences of such persons to the public never matter; what counts is the vested interest that enlarges them all sides including pot-bellies.

Thank God they ruling party even issued the approval to get the security personnel on duty. They might have thought they should just allow them after all they are brothers and sisters; same blood, same interests, identical feathers. The only difference is the nomenclature of the party.

The following day I left for work as God has enabled me to and while in transit you find this young man and woman both seated at the front and back of the taxi dozing and looking pale. A clear evidence that they didn't get enough sleep. And with the rush to get taxis and buses at night, many citizens get home late even though they are in the capital city with no major signs of natural traffic jams except for the artificially created ones like last night. This politics is too powerful.

The more you ignore politics, the more you underrate or overrate them, the more you keep feeling the heat of their actions and inactions and including their omissions and deliberate oversights. If politics is not working for your good, then it is working for your ill; no midpoint, explanations to it just black and white. Your level as a business executive or a struggling business does not exclude you from this traffic jam. It can put your family under stress if they are expecting you early or if you have picked your children from school hoping to be a good father/mother and drive them home in your car.

This is a pointer that politics can have a tremendous effect on your kitchen and the other room affairs. Denying it is risky, accepting it is telling you the truth and doing something about it is emancipating yourself from their claws. You are a citizen.

70.   HOW POLITICS AFFECTS YOU (3)

By the end of his first tenure, the executive of our state was seen as having delivered on the good promises of democracy (politics) with the help of cronies, in-laws and family. This was the appearance in the mind of people who were not on the ground in my state but the reality was that every project done by this government has dilapidated. The extent of dilapidation is at 105 % because they are burdens to the state, not needed, can't generate revenue after he has gone into retirement or God helps us to prosecute him.

People keep hearing of a certain State executive who is running with a bondage agenda rather than a rescue mission. Salaries are owed yet state weddings and birthdays are not phased out; in-laws are rewarded and even considered to take up the reins of leadership after the present executive is gone. We are being pillaged with lies of projects that are more than curses to us.

How do we explain that people who have worked and toiled with the various governments of past administration being left to suffer and giving their children the burden of planning burial when they can't even get jobs in the state? Who will rescue us with good deeds, not the bad one that is chaining us further? The lawmakers are puppets, more like zombies with the remote or whatever controlling them to do the bidding of one who is also endangering the future of their children. Can this curse be greater than the curse of God or is it too big for good men who fear God to resist the tyranny of a man who rose to leadership with a limp leg and corrupt philanthropy that is today eating up scarce state funds?

This evil in politics is too much for even the bad men to keep quiet yet the good seem not to even feel the effect is having on them and the ones it will have on their children. Do you not know that comfort zones are also hit with great calamity more than those in the open field of war? Power in the hands of rogues is being used to do perpetual evil, corruption that emanates from the deepest and lowest parts of hell and we stand, do nothing and mind a business that will be swept by this same storm and bad news.

My people, my people (I am not the governor), it is the time we make the corridors of power to hurt for occupation and habitation. A king that places himself at a level higher than God is reduced to the level where he will be converted to raw herbivore, consuming grass for the rest of their lives. No green pastures will be brought near them as they have dared to dehumanize the creatures of a Great and Mighty God.

Injustice (politics) has been meted out without remorse and now we must reward and convict bad governance without mercy.

71. THE LEADERSHIP GLASS CEILING OVER CITIZENS

The bane of Nigeria over the years have been described and blamed on a failure of leadership and Chinua Achebe of blessed memory told this expressly in his book; The Trouble with Nigeria. According to him, "The trouble with Nigeria is simply and squarely a failure of leadership. There is nothing basically wrong with the Nigerian character. There is nothing wrong with the Nigerian land or climate or water or air or anything else."

Nigeria's challenges are not about her citizens, the nature of our character, our climate, land or geographical topography because we are blessed with no challenges of volcanos, earthquakes and other hazardous natural disasters. The flooding experienced recently is a global climate change problem which we can handle and manage if the leadership really were proactive. Beyond the notion that our leaders don't come up with ideas, programs and initiatives to solve real problems, alleviate poverty, create equitable wealth and bring prosperity of the mind, soul and spirit, there is more to their failure.

We need to understand that the many failures of Nigerian leaders are not because they lack ideas, or don't understand our challenges and how to solve them. It is all deliberate, planned out and in fact a well-designed system to subjugate minds, create glass ceilings and make citizens be in constant survival modes of rat races that have been running for 50 years. From a recent Bishop T.D Jakes' interview with Pastor Steven Furtick, he said that we need to stop chasing chairs when God gave us trees to achieve much more with it.

The nature of the glass ceiling placed above us by our leadership is such that we are relegated to chasing daily bread when we can have abundance, wealth, systems that work, empires and ideas that can be sustained for many generations. When a man remembers that he needs to pay bills or woman remembers that a man is no longer an option to succeed we both are made to do all manner of jobs to make ends meet temporarily. Rather than having 10-year plans for ourselves and businesses we find people planning for festive seasons like Christmas, Sallah and various breaks that come up within a year.

Sadly, weekends are huge plans for many who feel they must enjoy the fruits of a week's hustle.

The strategy for imposing these glass ceilings

There is this dangerous narrative we have in Nigeria and many of such exist; that what you don't know does not kill you. Like it is better to be ignorant of something because with that you are safe. This is a lie that many have bought into, are living daily while those who know and know everything are scaling strange heights in their careers and businesses. Knowledge all through history has never been a curse even the wrong things have proved useful in many ways. Information and its importance have been seen as raw assets to build and execute any great idea.

The government and our leaders have succeeded in making education and whatever has to do with learning a frustration by mere thinking of reading, studying or lifelong learning. Education is where we have the many industrial strike actions. It is the tool of frustrating students to live idle lives, engages in crimes and frivolities, and become the workshop of evil deeds all designed by those we call leaders. The budget does not even make provision for funding the sector, it is corrupt to the point that teachers and lecturers are tools of further frustration on the students. They are not appreciated, rewarded or made to feel important or as shapers of destinies and leaders; so they relax and do what the system has conditioned them to do.

Education and good public enlightenment is a plus to any nation especially when citizens have a good measure or overdose of it. The knowledge of the world, of our ecosystem, of our true potentials and our rights as citizens. It is the man that knows and understands his rights that makes demands without being cowed or intimidated. Education is the greatest any government can offer her people if truly they care about growth, accountability, transparency and probity to those who elected them in a democracy.

The tool for glass ceiling above citizens by their governments is a system that makes them look but see less, a system that shields them from the big pictures of our potentials individually or collectively and places restrictions on good and healthy freedom of their people. They can afford to spend and burn monies that can close our minds rather than spend it to make us understand things they already know. Our knowledge, education and full enlightenment is a threat to their tyranny, dictatorship, bad and corrupt leadership that are clearly deliberate and selfish. If they can make education have its real effect then we would be a threat to their evil ways, we would confront them from a position of knowledge and equally apply the wisdom to change them when we are fed up.

The failure of our leadership is deliberate and they have succeeded to place citizens at a weak position where they can hardly do much by a denial of knowledge, learning, sound education and real exposure to what matters for growth.

72.   POST-NYSC   AND   YOUTH EXPECTATIONS

The compulsory National Youth Service Corps (NYSC) program for Nigerian graduates has over the years become unpopular for today's millennials. The structure and system that looks like a frustrated one year or a waste of time and resources make the NYSC look like a delay for the Nigerian youth. The days when people use to hope to serve their country with pride, dignity, honour and a sense of pride have faded away rapidly and the reasons are obvious. My desire is that this piece will address issues that affect corpers, before, during and after service year.

Points to Note

- The NYSC program was instituted to address a national challenge some 5 decades ago and unfortunately that challenge still is with us and the program has become a different shade of itself and more of failed bureaucratic edifice and configuration.
- While many hope it is phased out; you need to adapt and make the most of it while it lasts. Change the mindset of demonizing it and use it to better yourself, cash in opportunities and learn, unlearn, learn, relearn everything. Let it be a year of crash courses.
- Build networks, meet people for the right reasons for being better, improving yourself and building connections for concerted change.
- The time for youthful exuberance is gone; you are now an adult and needs to start thinking like one. Priorities should change (fun should not stop) but it should change position on your list.
- Don't fret, don't sink in the bad news about Nigeria. See the problems as opportunities for you to add value. Solutions are needed because there is a problem to be solved. Forget what they say of

recession, see it as an opportunity to work on an idea to bring the entire nation out of recession. We have many success stories too.

- You should decide where you desire to base and start a new life and phase. There are many reasons to choose a place but let it where you will add maximum value and get rewarded for it in monetary terms.

- Connect, network, attend events, go to free training, come to communal facilities, leave your comfort zone and explore the new territory. That is the only way you can create a good impression on people, prove your worth, and get a business card that will land your first job, contract and business idea.

- When the jobs don't come; start thinking of ideas, start searching for problems, go crazy about it, write them down, discuss with friends, mentors and colleagues. Let your mind not rest or stay idle; think, seek and search things out.

- Build your skills; the service should have been the best time to but is never too late. There are many free programs online and free events that will interest you. It is as these events that many capture ideas and open up new chapters for themselves. Volunteer as interns or in a charity or NGO.

- Believe in yourself, take the fear (of failure) away from you. This is not easy as I am writing it; you will need to work tirelessly to change that thinking that overwhelms you with fear and anxiety.
- There is nothing wrong with going for masters but choose something you will love to do or add value to your chosen career. Many first degrees are basic and along the line, many find new interests that come very easy to them.
- Enjoy life; be fulfilled, build a family, create your adventures and let no one belittle that ambition you have been nursing all your life.

It is your time, our time, the next generation and welcome to the world of making positive changes. NYSC is over, life begins and you need courage, strength, character and every virtue to succeed. Nigeria is grateful for your national service (NYSC).

73.   AYO FAYOSE'S DECLARATION AND THE LIMITS OF DEMOCRACY

Governor Ayo Fayose of Ekiti is one man that is characterized by many controversies that emanate from the political scene in Nigeria. These controversies are matched with the courage of his words, actions, inactions, speeches and engagement on national issues. Love him or hate him, see him as a hypocrite or not, Ayodele Peter Fayose speaks some truths when he opens his mouth. He has declared for President in 2019 and his party the People's Democratic Party is venting and telling him to stop wasting his time.

Nigeria and her political stakeholders have been playing politics of zoning and sharing power among the various constituent elements of the country. History has it on record that the Northern region has had the longest-serving times leading this country. Reason being that they have the population swing the block votes for any Presidential elections that it took someone like MKO Abiola to defy such odds even with a Muslim-Muslim ticket in 1993.

The struggle for power in Nigeria and grabbing it comes with a lot of calculation that needs to weigh the preponderance of one group over another. The north has always got the larger share but without prejudice to the Northern brothers and sisters; the North is made up of various ethnic groups beyond the popular Hausa-Fulani or Muslim groups. This applies to the Southern region as well; however, the North still got the landmass and population.

It is clear that any time a party in the opposition wants to take over power or look relevant at the election outcome, they will float a Northern candidate with the needed popularity among the unrecorded population of humans and otherwise. The main opposition party the PDP is towing similar paths despite the 1999 understanding rotating the President first among the major ethnic groups.

We have a constitution that everyone has the right to run for any office in the country so long as he/she has met the minimum requirements and with the recent reviews made more people are qualified to run the office when age is considered. The idea of zoning, however, is party arrangement started by the PDP and Nigerians are hardly part of the process of picking party flagbearers yet they keep picking them and make us vote for hopeless choices. How are we sure that Governor Ayo Peter Fayose cannot put an on a faster path to growth and here we are having his party trying to make his ambition irrelevant.

Mind you; this piece is not an endorsement of Ayo Fayose or whatever his affiliations might be or where he stands on national issues but to show us that Nigerians are being further pushed to the point of not being a part of the key decisions to elect leaders. The Presidency and the office are now at the mercy of secret meetings with many oaths sworn without Nigerians being let in on it. Not even the media has details of what happens in those meetings or the exchanges that take place and here we are preaching good governance for Nigeria.

The story is not far of how a group of governors held a President to ransom in the name of his previous undocumented agreement not to run for a second term and we claim to be running a democracy. What really is the definition of our democracy if a group of sectional leaders with various interests decide to foist a President on us Nigerians? Why should an Ayo Fayose run the risk of being disqualified not on the basis of incompetence or corruption or otherwise but because he is not from the North or the zoning arrangement does not include this section of the country? This is clearly not a democracy or anything close to it or maybe something Africa should be proud of.

Back to the same old rhythm.

The same rhythm why we need to go back a bit lower and review our founding laws, principles and national aspirations. The rhythm why many people think that the present system is clearly not working for all or is it healthy for good, solid, sound ideas to work and thrive. The same rhythm why restructuring has become the most popular word in the last 2 years yet we are getting ready to go to the polls like that. This democracy needs a review and a change to a modus operandi that is humane and does not choke its citizens who truly want to work hard and succeed.

We need a democracy where people (like Ayo Fayose) are not made to reduce their aspirations or feel marginalized because of a selfish clause in a party constitution, not drafted by Nigerians or a majority of us. It is either the democracy works for us all or we change the name to something more description so we can no our realities. Telling us it is a democracy when clearly it isn't is an insult to every educated Nigerian and effort to lie to all of the people all of the time.

74.   ASO ROCK CABALS: NO LONGER IN GUY FAWKES MASK

I really don't know if Guy Fawkes is the right person to qualify the Aso Rock Cabals but seeing the present ones promised change; Guy Fawkes also and his colleagues in England desired to change the events happening in their time. Guy Fawkes and his beliefs have been depicted in the contemporary movie, V for Vendetta; great movie. According to him, violence can be used as a force for good to exterminate those who didn't mean well for the people and blowing up ancient buildings like Parliament buildings.

Talking of the Aso Rock Cabals and the many things we don't know about our seat of government, it won't out of place to seek for an overhaul of the spirit-haunted Aso Villa of the Nigerian President. Is it possible to burn it down to ashes and build something worthy and accessible to the people of Nigeria?

For the undoing of the Aso Rock Cabals; we didn't start hearing about them today. They have been there and in fact, Nigeria is not the first country worth people who practically design and manage the operations in the corridors of government and political power. America's version is those found on Wall Street who practically are the shareholders of the White House in a near decent way.

The Nigerian version was known to be operating in secrecy; they don't come out in public, neither do they own to recalling a looter still on the run but today they have become brazenly courageous to display their identities. Cabals are no longer business people with special interests of controlling stakes in the business or economic sector, they are now at the decision-making table of second-guessing the President and undermining the Ag. President.

So if you are to define who an Aso Rock Cabal is what will it be?

The cabal can be seen as a group of persons and individuals who have the power to make the President feel like a figure, possibly sign his signature and turn the President to a President in denial. Such powers I bet you are powerful and equally potent to crumble every democratic institution that we are making efforts. When one of them is able to recall someone charged with looting of funds, you will agree with me that his confidence is backed by something bigger than the entire Aso Rock, the offices and people there.

Where lies the powers of the Office of the President of Africa's most populous nation? Why is that office being undermined in ways that bring embarrassment at home and abroad?

The entire institutions of our democracy are under threat if we can keep on having individuals defy our supreme lies and get away with it. When a vocal directive and unverified signatures hold much power than what is understood to be the responsibility of certain institutions under the Presidency, then fire is really on Aso Rock.

Individuals have succeeded in making their powers supersede those of institutions and stipulated laws, and for how long? Aso Rock cabals need to be shown the power of our democracy and the powers vested in Nigerian citizens.

75.   POPULISM IN POLITICS: NIGERIA'S VERSION

The concept of populism or acceptable opinion and views has engulfed the politics around the world. From America to France, to Germany, to East Africa, Catalonia and Nigeria; more politicians are winning the heart of the people by tapping into their strength and weaknesses. Populism thrives on the perception of what people think of themselves, far from what truth says.

President Trump rose to power on the platform of America First, Make America Great Again, he came to give priority to America and Americans who felt that their place in the world is denying them honour at home. The populism in politics reached France this year with the emergence of an Independent from the Socialist Party Emmanuel Macron to be the nation's youngest President in history. Yes, the youth and young people phrases are populists in nature.

In Nigeria, President Buhari came with the corruption mantra understanding fully that Nigerians see corruption only in their leaders. And with the prevailing sad times of Boko Haram, he marched swiftly to Aso Rock as a former general and war veteran. The rest we are always told is history.

Populism in Politics as it concerns Nigeria reflects both during the elections and why governance is going on. I will dwell on certain cases where politicians have swayed the voters with talks that are appealing to their conscious and the subconscious. It is the most viable campaign strategy that modern and contemporary politics has evolved to and adopted as well. You simply appeal to their emotions or think like them, say something that makes them feel good or whatever the larger opinion is against the incumbent.

Stomach Infrastructure

The above nomenclature came into Nigeria's socio-political space when the Ekiti State Governor Ayo Fayose defeated a sitting governor of the State, Kayode Fayemi to return as the Governor of Ekiti State, Nigeria. The idea and strategy were simple; feed the people, food is a daily need that requires daily struggles and with a long history of bad leadership they people are reduced to struggle daily. The Rat race that makes people to be reduced to survival mode is what Stomach Infrastructure came to meet. He shared indomie, rice and basic food items that the downtrodden didn't have access to and with their population and him speaking their language he got the popular votes and got elected.

Stomach infrastructure and other like activities of food sharing dwell basically on the vulnerability of the people and inability/struggle to get a daily meal. A crook who is a politician does not mind dining with the poor for the election period and because they are more in population, a day or two meals worth is the tool of populism.

Biafra & Anambra

Biafra and the recent agitations by the Indigenous People of Biafra (IPOB) gained traction among the common man in the South-Eastern States including Anambra. In fact, one of the contenders for the November 16th gubernatorial elections Mr Osita Chidoka drove Nnamdi Kanu from prison when he was released. His body language has shown that he clearly is sympathetic to Nnamdi Kanu's cause but he won't take the boycotting of elections in Anambra State. He was also at the recent hearing in court where Nnamdi Kanu has gone MIA (missing in action) and needs to be produced in court.

In a deliberate landmark declaration of campaign open, Mr Osita Chidoka chose Uli to do this and that is clearly populist to Biafra. What is special about the town Uli? Uli was used as the airstrip/airport where planes (over 3000) that arrived Biafra during the war. It was designed in such a way that they were covered with palm fronds to confuse the Nigerian air forces. However, when a plane sympathetic to Biafra like bringing supplies arrives and the men on the ground are notified the palm fronds will be removed and lights came on everywhere in on the strip.

Uli airstrip was one of the inventions and creativity of war that Ojukwu inspired in Biafra. So, Mr Osita Chidoka is truly a politician who equally understands the time. If by tomorrow you find a politician going to the same location of the Asaba massacre to solicit for votes or launch a campaign you will understand what they are trying to appeal to.

Nigeria's version of populism in politics though gaining ground takes up a shade that makes the politician look saintly, passionate and a thoughtful leader but it all turned out badly. Free education, unfortunately, is being peddled to lure young people and their aged parents to feel butterflies of emotions of having a messiah that has come to rescue them.

Populism and the many shades that it comes in are fueled by the desperation of the people to have better lives. They have crossed the red line of having their honour intact so their votes and support are now for sale. A plate of indomie is rich enough to sell off birthrights of human dignity, access to water, health, education and what other contemporary nations offer their democracies.

We need to educate people. They need enlightenment and patience to tarry a little while to have a good man/woman in office. Anambra is at the front burner of deciding how the real match in 2019 will be like and we just launched a platform that will be used to engage politicians before the elections by examining their manifestos and promises.

PollsJuror.com has the vision to shape elections using data. It can be economic data, demographic data, revenue data, global and local market data, education data, health data and all these will be matched with the promises made by politicians in their manifestos.

76.   THE INFAMY OF ROCHAS OKOROCHA

The people's governor Rochas Okorocha has evolved from a philanthropist to a widely accepted governor of the masses (with a rescue mission) to a governor who is trying to recoup back his philanthropic investments in Imo state, Nigeria. It sounds more like that Gladiator movie of the General who became a slave, a slave who became a Gladiator and a Gladiator who defied an Emperor; a great story isn't but the major difference here is that the latter was in strength and honour.

The purpose of this piece, therefore, is to curate the transition of Rochas Okorocha to what he is today and if time permits I can draw some conclusions on why it looks like the governor is about to have political career terminated. It could well mean he understands this so he is learning the ropes again in being a philanthropist digitally. (Remember his Twitter You are very stupid of Japheth Omojuwa's tweet).

I remember vividly the coming of Rochas Okorocha to Awo-Omamma in Imo state. That day, the stretch from 33' Consolidated Breweries Plc. to Awo junction was filled with people cheering the APGA candidate as he enjoyed his Keke ride. (He is a master of populism too). This, was after Imo people rejected Governor Ikedi Ohakim who was alleged to have given a tacit approval of harassing a . Catholic Reverend Father. That unfortunately for him landed him the object of the black mass procession by Catholics in Imo State (and other parts of the world) and unfortunately gave us what Obasanjo's described as Imo people choosing an "Armed Robber over small thief."

In his inaugural speech, the man Anayo proved that he is one hell of an orator; I practically loved him for that. His combination of Igbo rhymes with the English language is second to none and on that day the free education program was declared. The chanting of young people and their parents increased as the messiah has lifted the burden of school fees from them. The opening of roads closed by Ohakim and erecting of structures, expansion of roundabouts, a landmark of irrelevant projects like the many decorations that occupy the space that people should be using in Owerri.

Rochas also made revelations of how the previous governments deposit workers' money in the bank and accrue profit from it and Imo workers were angry and happy with Rochas for this revelation. Fast forward to 2017; which is better money deposited for profit or money used to erect statues.

Then came to issue of ADAPALM which he renamed IMO Palm Plantation. Now the former name did not make it less Imo rather Rochas needed to add that to his CV that he renamed it that. The gospel of palm fruits started, ***Ikuola nkwu*** (have you planted your palm). Rochas was telling the young and old to start owning their own palm trees for the next generation and Imo people including myself were impressed. 5 years after Imo Palm Plantation is now a darker shadow of what it was before the coming of Governor Rochas. To conclude this part, the many projects in the state; of roads and streetlights have contractors being owed for works that the governor asked them to finish if they must get paid.

The projects are now dilapidated. I mean every project that was done by Rochas in the first tenure has reached 101 percent dilapidation. Contractors are owed, the users of the road don't enjoy the roads, pensioners are being owed for over 70 months (5 years plus). Interestingly, when they demanded their pensions, Rochas asked these aged people why they didn't train children that will look after them at old age.

Are we not in an interesting democracy under Rochas Okorocha? Where lies the heart of which he was using to do humanitarian projects if he could speak the grandparents and parents of the children he might be helping through school (or relatives for those who are orphaned). Rochas planned to build new hospitals (which he did) but also went further to engage private practitioners to take over the old ones and run it so those who have worked there for years will lose their jobs or receive demeaning treatment.

Thankfully, the union protested, Rochas lost out, the new hospitals are occupied by weeds and rodents and the health workers have been receiving half salaries for 2 years without leave allowance for them. You could call it a vendetta for going against the people's governor who now is changing colours to the tyrannical monarch. Speaking of monarchs, Rochas in his way of practising federalism introduced a fourth-tier of government or the second tier for his state; the traditional leadership stool.

Going deeper, you will find that the free education that he proclaimed on May 29, 2011, is actually a fiction; students still pay to be in the schools in IMO. Either they are being levied by school authorities because the governor has not been paying or the standard is terribly at an all-time low. Rochas has taken the face of billboards to a whole new level; he approved contracts to put his face shaking hands with Obama and if you ask the 44th President of the United States he might denying he can't remember shaking hands with him (even with the pictures). Do you think that if Rochas tries to get familiar with President Obama at the airport now that the Secret Service agents will let him get close?

Rochas has celebrated his birthday, foundation and everything about him more than he has celebrated IMO people or whatever that concerns them. He has also resorted to bullying on social media, engaging in hate speech thereby crossing the red line.

The sins of Rochas are many and to draw conclusions on the Infamy of Rochas Anayo Okorocha let me point out the following;

- Populism is a danger to any democracy.
- Oratory does not equal performance in leadership.
- Not all businessmen are actually business people. They are simply contractors; buying and supply. That is what Rochas is and not even a Philanthropist. Have you found out how he got money to finance the projects? Have you asked why he has not spoken about the NGO bill?
- IMO people need to wake up and challenge every bad government that seeks to reduce to penury and servitude.
- Rochas still thinks he can be the President of Nigeria; ***onyi isi ala Nigeria***. Why do you think he moved to the APC? He hopes that he will be that Igbo President that we have for long hoped for?
- No project done by Rochas can boast of 80 percent success rate whether it is in completion or adding

value to the people. They will either leave us in debt or keep incurring costs.

- Rochas plans to Imo to a monarchy by his plans handover to a son-in-law.

Like said his sins and many and for the many useless and unproductive things he did while causing people to lose their lives and means of livelihood, his political career is ended. Anyone connected to his family tree will have that tag of Rochas who erected a statue of President Jacob Zuma who is uncelebrated in his country South Africa. Meanwhile, the next governor will need to bring it down for people to recover from the trauma of Rochas' administration or whatever is tied to such ugly projects. A total reversal.

I am equally sad to think that IMO people have never had it better after Sam Mbakwe (Dee Sam) left office. *Ala Imo nwere mmadu, ola ebe ha no?*

Thank you (for the lessons) Excellency Governor Rochas Anayo Okorocha and no thanks.

77.   NIGERIA'S MILLENNIAL AND INDEPENDENT CANDIDACY

The young people of Nigeria seem not to understand the times as much as they are expected to; we are more concerned about social media ranting. Each one desires to score a point that is always never near political correctness. We desire to change and a good one at that and in the peak of many historical events the Independent Candidacy bill passed in the National Assembly yet we are involved in online squabbles that gather likes, lols and retweets.

In Hong Kong, the person leading the revolution for the young people is 21 and he started about 4 years. He has been to prison for it and yesterday he was released alongside a fellow activist Nathan Law who is 24 years old. The many strategies of the past have failed and as a country in a democratic setting and dispensation, we need something civil, democratic and cannot be pushed back by the enemies among us.

Two bills were passed some months ago and they are particularly gains for the youth population; Not Too Young to Run bill and the Independent Candidacy Bill. The age for contesting elections was reduced and Independent Candidacy can now run for elections without belonging to any political party or organization.

This is a development that is not just good but equally timely. We are in a time where people are losing jobs, compromising for money, selling their bodies for money, taking their lives yet our potential for greatness has not diminished since 1960. The same strategy is still in use for managing our commonwealth and the enemies of egalitarian prosperity keep giving excuses why the system will or cannot work. With the highest population of youths in Africa, Nigeria's potential is the weight of her young people. A shake-up of the young population is a shake-up for Africa.

Independent Candidacy and the Battle of Two Generations

A section of the country and into various categorization have hijacked the instruments of the state and national institutions as their personal tool of many ills that stink to the high heavens. They are using it to favour their cronies, <u>expand territories of wealth</u>, influence and power for their generations yet unborn. All these are done on the backdrop of the sweat and hard work of others. Many (of these hard working people) have lost dignity in the workplace and at home.

My wish is that the young people like myself will realize that this fight is simply of old values, generation and thinking and one of the new values, better systems and thinking. The world of the youth has gone geometrically in a progressive manner. Technology has proved that we can superior to the old generation (and they should be proud of this), but no; keeping us in a convoluted rat race all year is a perfect strategy.

It is time to close ranks and understand the nature of the struggle for the soul of our country. It is time to develop a strategy that cannot be faulted solely to take up our country for those who pillage us every day.

These days you don't need anyone to tell us that everything is wrong with those stirring the ship of this African giant. As much as they cannot have the monopoly of understanding about governance, they are defying principles and values with impunity that sets new records. Reports from our seat of our power Aso Rock are either incoherent; defies commonsense, controversial, fake, uncalculated, embarrassing, treasonable and a grave risk for the future.

My Proposition

We have the Independent Candidacy, Not Too Young to run the bill, resources and a population that guarantees over the years the power of our collective votes. As we work to close ranks and understand the nature of this struggle let's choose for ourselves candidates that will run in 2019.

Strategy for 2019?

The form for Presidential elections was sold for 21 million right? That could have been deliberate to keep young people from elective offices. We today have the 'Not Too Young to Run' bill, we have Independent Candidacy bill. These two mean that we can't be frustrated by political parties and the glass ceiling of age is lifted.

Close ranks and choose our candidates as young people (over 80 million). Crowdfund, raise money and float our candidates and power is taken back democratically from one generation to another. The Independent Candidacy bill can be a tool of our liberation if we plan and work towards it.

#Amandla □

78.   SHADES OF FEMINISTS

A quick disclaimer will be good for such a piece and with this kind of topic; in fact, I want to admit to being a feminist but a selective one. I leave you to decipher what I mean but looking for clarification on the selective part, feel free to buzz me.

I got to learn about feminism and what it portrays after discovering the person of Chimamanda Adichie; a great writer and feminist whom I have come to admire. Her presentation (We should all be feminist) on the popular TED talks was nothing short of intellectual, smart and highly intelligent. Talking of intellectualism I can now delve into the first shade of feminists.

Before I continue with this piece let me recall the definition that Adichie gave for a feminist; a person who believes in the sexual, political, racial and economic equality of the sexes. Equality is the key word there but that definition does not talk more about how one should preach about or crusade about feminism, even though in the full speech she mention personal experiences.

Now to my first shade or feminism classification.

Those who through determination and willpower distinguished themselves in their chosen fields of endeavour. Those who defied every odd or notion that it is a man's world to achieve tremendous feats legitimately and graciously, with no compromise of the moral values that society recognize. They are heroes and mentors for both men and women alike. They drive intellectual discourse in their various nations and continents. These ones are partners with men in the shaping of our world.

I doff my hat for them every day.

When you have a woman about to become the President of the most powerful nation on earth and her antecedents, you can understand the category of women I am trying to describe here. Those are the truest of feminists backed up with the right societal values of hard work, diligence, dedication and courage.

Above all these descriptions; their intellect has worked and is what works for them.

To the next shade.

It is unfortunate that the world is such that women are mostly at the receiving end of different discrimination; sexual assault, harassment, relationship heartbreaks, issues of single parents or mothers, the resultant effect of a runaway dad on the girls (when the mum is not able to inculcate the right values), etc. Let me state that many come out of this circumstances and become role models to others while some other allow it bring out a personality that abhors the masculine gender.

So when a young lady has built her mentality that all men mistreat women, what you get is a kind of feminism that isn't healthy. They become defensive, hateful with words, arrogant, annoyingly rude and unnecessarily outspoken even when no one cares to hear.

From this piece, I can only classify feminists into two broad categories of those who advocate for women on the right values and those who do that on the wrong values. The values of success are always constant but the paths might vary but for the wrong values they vary based on each person's experience.

The society now has those who went through molestation of different kinds, the ones who have endured heartbreaks that turn them against the men they once loved, family separations, rape, sexual harassment, unhealthy advances when it comes to work-related issues and a whole lot. Each person that has one hard feeling against the male folks has definitely had one unique experience or the other.

Women are great personalities and they are part of what makes a world that use to be a man's world more beautiful. Treating them right is not too much to ask seeing that make this man's world more beautiful. My selective feminism is borne on the premise that I will defend those ones who are worth defending. Those ones who are worth being treated as queens by the kings of this world. Those ones whose intellects arouse the loins of any man.

They are the MVPs of feminism. For those who have inculcated wrong notions about men; life experiences are there for us to learn good lessons not to change us from lovers to haters. The world is full of bad people and if you get to the wrong hands, it doesn't mean the rest people (men) are all bad. We all can be one republic. Never!

If there is anything the world needs, it is more female role models if for nothing else for the sake of the daughter(s) I would have. I desire that they inculcate right values to live life to the fullest.

Cheers to the women inspire us to do more!

79.   THIS IS YOUR TIME

The world we find ourselves in is indeed a dynamic, changing and a progressive one. Men and women have been privileged to pass through it- of varying sizes, opinions, convictions, visions for the world, race, nations, tribes, ideas, values and philosophies. Some left indelible marks made generational impacts that can't be forgotten; some others lived it casually and carelessly. In essence, a passage through this world is an opportunity to play a role in making the world better.

Martin Luther King Jnr. in one of his many inspiring speeches, made some remarkable statements that if God gave him a choice to come to this world in any period he desires, he would still come back to the 1960s (a period characterized by racial discrimination and civil rights movement). He said he would turn down an offer to be born in the time of Aristotle or Plato but would be glad to fight the good fight of restoring the dignity of Blacks in America (Protestants and Catholics, Jews and Gentiles).

I have heard many people wish they were born in a particular century or time, thinking things would have been better, but come to think of it, you think Nelson Mandela would have many roles to play in a South Africa without apartheid or Martin Luther the 14th century reformer would have much impact if there was no need in the church. It would have been either they are overwhelmed in the midst of a greater challenge or had no influence at all.

A generation is enough and full of problems for people to meet such challenges.

For us in the 21st century, challenges abound, needs are everywhere, so many things have to be corrected. Therefore, opportunities are enormous for anybody and everybody to make an impact. Also, I have heard people that wish to change the world and make it better, as good as that may sound, there is little or a part you can play. Even if you make the world near perfect in your lifetime, when you are gone fresh challenges will arise and you won't be there to keep changing the world. Climate change and sustainable development were not an issue 20 years ago.

The world is dynamic and progressive and it is that nature that has brought you here (in this century) to solve that challenge that wasn't present 20 years ago. It is a season of opportunities and it is also limited, therefore there is need to maximize it.

Your time for impact is now, and for this generation.